REVERSE CRESCENT KICK

Achieving Kicking Excellence™

Shawn Kovacich

TM

AUTHOR APPROVED ADVANCE COPY

Printed in the United States of America

Library of Congress Card Number: 2004090162

ISBN #0-9707496-4-3

Table of Contents

Disclaimer

Please note that the author and/or publisher of this instructional book are **Not Responsible** in any manner whatsoever, for any injury, which may occur by reading and/or following the instructions located within this book. The techniques described within this book are sophisticated in nature and have the potential to cause serious damage to the reader or readers, if performed incorrectly. Therefore, it is essential that the reader or readers of this book consult a qualified and competent physician before following any of the activities, physical or otherwise, which are described within this book. This book is intended to be used as a supplemental training aid, and should be used as such, under the guidance of a qualified and competent martial arts instructor.

Copyrights & Trademarks

Acknowledgements

I would like to take this opportunity to thank the following individuals who were the first students I had that received their black belts under my instruction. It was truly and honor and a privilege to have had you as my students.

Dick Allen

Chris Eamon

Rick Johns

Ed Perro

Henry Smith

This book would never have been published without the assistance of the following people who have contributed their time, energy, and skill in the creation of this book.

Doug and Cassie Bender for the use of their facility used in principle photography.

The staff and owners of Sports West Gym for the use of their facility and equipment used in principle photography.

Jessica Bronder for her assistance, and Ron Dunlap for his participation in this book.

"Before I studied the art, a punch to me was just a punch, a kick was just a kick. After I studied the art, a punch was no longer a punch, a kick was no longer a kick. Now that I understand the art, a punch is just a punch, a kick is just a kick." —Bruce Lee

About the Author

Watching Shawn Kovacich teach is like watching a college professor explaining quantum physics in such a way, that it is as easily understandable as a current episode of Sesame Street. With his unique ability to analyze and break down any kick to its most basic level, he then explains in exacting detail, the important aspects of each and every component in the kick. This gives the student a complete and detailed analysis of every movement in the kick from beginning to end.

Mr. Kovacich started his martial arts training at the age of seventeen, and took to it like the proverbial duck to water, earning his first-degree black belt after two years and nine months of training. His teaching ability became evident early on in his training and he often assisted his instructors with newer students.

The most influential moment of Mr. Kovacich's early martial arts training came when he was privileged to not only witness, but also to participate in two of his instructors, Shihan Brian Knechtges and Sensei Ben Hunn's, third degree black belt test, in which Shihan Knechtges and Sensei Hunn had to fight continuously for 100 minutes each against a fresh opponent every minute. Punches and kicks were not pulled and the two men were pushed beyond all normal standards of human endurance. Both men not only prevailed and were awarded their third degree black belts, but they also became a source of inspiration for Mr. Kovacich. Years later, he would take this test not once, but twice, and emerged triumphant both times.

Shortly after testing for and receiving his first-degree black belt, Mr. Kovacich accomplished another prestigious goal while participating in a charity fund-raiser. That goal, which he easily reached, was the first of what was to become two world records for endurance high kicking certified by The Guinness Book of World Records.

Mr. Kovacich has been an active instructor, teaching in as many as three schools at a time since 1985. He has taught students of all ages from six to sixty-eight, and from all walks of life, including law enforcement personnel, military personnel, correctional officers, mental health professionals, etc. Since the early 90's, he has also been an active competitor in bare knuckle full-contact karate. Competing in such prestigious tournaments throughout the United States such as the Sabaki Challenge, the Great Northwest Sabaki Satellite, the U.S. Shidokan Open, and the Shidokan Team USA. Mr. Kovacich still actively competes in these tournaments as well as being one of the top Instructor/Coaches for the former USTU (United States Tae Kwon Do Union) national and international tae kwon do competitions.

Mr. Kovacich is currently a fourth-degree black belt in both Karate and Tae Kwon Do. Powerful and intelligent, he is constantly analyzing every movement in a kick in order to get the most speed and power available. He is one of only a handful of instructors who can improve anyone's kicking ability regardless of their physical ability or non-ability, or their martial arts style. Unyielding power is what makes Shawn Kovacich a world-class fighter, but what makes him truly unique is his analytical and innovative teaching ability.

Preface

In an unarmed self-defense encounter, your kicking skills or lack thereof, can be the deciding factor between victory and defeat. I can still remember back in my high school days when kicking was considered dirty fighting, and seldom if ever used. Things certainly have changed since the late 70's and early 80's. Today kicking is not only used more frequently, but it also ranks as perhaps the most versatile and underrated weapon that you have in your personal arsenal. With the noted exception of your head, and I don't mean as a physical weapon, but in your ability to intelligently avoid the threat, and if you are unable to avoid it, to overcome it as quickly and efficiently as possible.

Presented here are several different reasons why you should learn and practice the kicking skills presented not only in this book, but also from a certified and competent martial arts instructor.

1. The majority of people do not know how to kick, and therefore tend to rely mainly on their hands, giving them only two weapons. By learning how to kick, you have doubled your available weapons from two (your hands) to four (your hands and feet).
2. Your legs are the most powerful physical weapons that you have in your arsenal. They are several times stronger than your arms and have a greater reach.
3. Kicking can be your "Ace in the Hole" when fighting. Used properly, your opponent will not expect it and will never know what hit him.
4. Kicking adds another dimension to your fighting abilities by allowing you to kick at the same time your hands are defending, attacking or grabbing your opponent.
5. If you wind up on the ground, kicking can give you that extra split second in order to keep your opponent at bay while you regain your standing position. And finally,
6. Kicking helps keep you in shape by constantly strengthening and stretching the legs and lower torso. It is all too easy to forget that your legs are carrying you around everyday. Without them where would you be?

The exact reason why you have decided to begin utilizing the kicking skills taught in this book depends upon your own personal needs and interests. You may enjoy it because of the stress reduction and physical fitness benefits, or simply because you enjoy the physical challenge that kicking correctly presents. While others enjoy the sporting, or competition aspects of the tournament arena. However for most people, their primary reason for practicing these kicking skills is for self-defense.

Irregardless of the reason, the materials presented in this book are beneficial to anyone who wants to improve their kicking ability, whether it is the martial artist, tournament competitor, aerobic kick-boxing enthusiast, or the self-defense advocate.

While this book and the material presented within it are invaluable to the individual who does not have the opportunity to learn in a formal setting, it is also a tremendous benefit to those who are fortunate enough to have access to a qualified and competent instructor. A privilege and an honor one should never take for granted.

It is my hope that every person who picks up this book and studies it, walks away with an in-depth understanding of how to correctly perform all of the intricate aspects of the Back Leg Reverse Crescent Kick and its 10 most common variations. As the individual becomes increasingly proficient at performing their kicking and fighting skills, their need to exercise self-discipline, self-control, and responsibility increases dramatically.

What exactly is a Reverse Crescent Kick?

I am often asked this question and the best response that I have come up with is simply this, "A properly executed Reverse Crescent Kick performed by a man (or woman), is likened to the backhand swing of a tennis player hitting a tennis ball across the net." As you look at the illustration of the tennis player below, imagine executing a Reverse Crescent Kick with your right leg in a clockwise motion (striking from the inside of your body towards the outside), just like the tennis player backhanding the tennis ball with his tennis racket utilizing his right hand.

Note:

All of the kicks shown in this book were executed with the right leg. Therefore, in order to execute these kicks with the left leg, simply switch each kicks description from left to right and vice versa where appropriate. I have included a complete description of Switch Turning Reverse Crescent Kick utilizing the left leg at the end of the Back Leg Reverse Crescent Kick Variations chapter. Use this as a guideline for switching the description of the other kicks for use with the left leg.

How To Use This Book

Although you can learn all of the techniques shown in this book on your own, there are many different subtleties and variables present within each of the kicks shown that true mastery of any of these kicks can only be gained under the knowledgeable eye of a qualified and competent instructor. This book is designed to be a reference manual for the instructor, and a textbook for the student. In order to learn from this book, you must first grasp a basic understanding on how to learn. In explaining this, I like to use the story of learning how to walk.

Every one of us, you included, came into this world as a baby. Did you run marathons as a baby? Of course not. You weren't even able to do anything for yourself, except for maybe making messes. And everybody has been through that, no matter whom or what they are, we all started out as babies. Now how does a baby first get around? Does he walk or run? No, of course not, a baby first gets around by being carried. Then as the baby's muscles get stronger and he gets a little older he starts to crawl. And in no time at all, he gets pretty good at it and watch out. He is all over the place in no time at all and seemingly faster than greased lightning. After awhile, crawling gets kind of old and he begins to start learning how to walk. Mom and Dad are their holding his hand as he staggers across the room like a drunken sailor on a Saturday night.

Of course there are the falls and spills that happen as he tries walking on his own, but such is the process of learning. After a while he starts walking on his own and then comes the baby run, which if you are a parent or have ever baby sat a small child you know exactly what I am talking about. It begins with you looking away for just a second and then bang, he's off like a thoroughbred at the Kentucky Derby going for the Triple Crown, and almost as fast. Eventually the baby grows into a child and learns how to run and jump and do all kinds of things.

Of course none of these would have been possible if he hadn't first been carried, then taught to crawl, and had his hand held as he learned to walk, and perhaps just as important, received all those bumps and bruises from falling down and getting back up and trying it again.

The key to learning from this book is to be patient, start slow and take it in steps. Don't skip steps or rush the learning process. Years went into the making of this book in order to give you the best possible source of information on how to correctly execute the kicks presented within.

Go to the Doctor:
You should always consult with a qualified and competent physician before trying any of the techniques described in this book.

Read:
Take this book and read it cover to cover several times, before attempting to execute any of the techniques presented in this book.

Study and Learn:
Learn the who, what, where, when, why and how's of the anatomy and principles behind the kicks presented in this book. Remember that ignorance may be

bliss, but knowledge truly is power.

Warm-Up and Stretching:

Always warm-up and stretch thoroughly and properly before participating in any physical activity. An ounce of prevention is worth a pound of cure.

Take One Step at a Time:

When writing this book, I designed it so that each kick was broken down into several different sections with several technical points in each section. All of this was done so that you could full understand how to correctly execute each of the 11 kicks presented. With the understanding that once you had learned all of the technical points in each section, that you would then put them all together until you were able to perform each movement in every section of the kick as one continuous movement.

Let's use the primary kick Back Leg Reverse Crescent Kick as an example, now the best way to understand this is to look at it on a mathematical level. By this I mean that you are going to learn this kick on a $1 + 1 = 2$ level. Each number one is representative of a technical point that is included in each section. For example Fighting Position has seven technical points. Here is what I mean.

1. Position of your feet = 1
2. Position of your knees = 1
3. Position of your upper body = 1
4. Position of your hands and elbows = 1
5. Position of your back = 1
6. Position of your head = 1
7. Position of your eyes = 1

For a total of 7 technical points.

Now when you look at all of the technical points in each section of a Back Leg Reverse Crescent Kick, it would look like this.

Fighting Position = $1 + 1 + 1 + 1 + 1 + 1 + 1 = 7$
Begin Arc = $1 + 1 + 1 + 1 + 1 + 1 + 1 + 1 = 8$
Peak of Arc = $1 + 1 + 1 + 1 + 1 + 1 + 1 + 1 = 8$
Impact = $1 + 1 + 1 + 1 + 1 + 1 + 1 + 1 = 8$
Follow Through = $1 + 1 + 1 + 1 + 1 + 1 + 1 + 1 = 8$
End of Arc = $1 + 1 + 1 + 1 + 1 + 1 + 1 + 1 = 8$
Return to Fighting Position = $1 + 1 + 1 + 1 + 1 + 1 + 1 = 7$

For a total of 54 technical points.

What this book was designed to do was to have you fully practice each section until each of the technical points in each section becomes second nature to you. Then you will go onto the next section and do the same thing until you have learned each of the technical points in each section. After that has been accomplished, you will then put each of the sections together one at a time until you are able to perform the entire sequence of movements correctly. For example:

1. Fighting Position
2. Fighting Position + Begin Arc
3. Fighting Position + Begin Arc + Peak of Arc

4. Fighting Position + Begin Arc + Peak of Arc + Impact
5. Fighting Position + Begin Arc + Peak of Arc + Impact + Follow Through
6. Fighting Position + Begin Arc + Peak of Arc + Impact + Follow Through + End of Arc
7. Fighting Position + Begin Arc + Peak of Arc + Impact + Follow Through + End of Arc + Return to Fighting Position

Ideally you should execute any kick without conscious thought and in one single fluid motion. The execution of the kick should be instinctive in nature rather than an action or reaction, which in both cases are infinitely slower than acting instinctively. However just like a baby, you must first go through the entire learning process until executing the kick becomes as natural and without thought as breathing.

Learn the Primary Kick First:

This is pretty much self-explanatory, since everything else is based on the Back Leg Reverse Crescent Kick. Once you learn this primary kick, all of the other variations will be much easier to learn and execute.

Practice, Practice, Practice:

I have heard it said that one must practice any given technique 1,000 times before they know it. I totally and completely disagree. You should correctly practice any technique 3,000 to 5,000 times to learn it, 10,000 times correctly to know it, and a lifetime of practice to master it.

Read this book regularly:

Use this book as a reference guide on a regular basis. As a general rule-of-thumb, every time you practice a Reverse Crescent Kick 1,000 times you should have read this book at least once.

Quality Supervision:

Whenever possible, you should always practice under the watchful eye of a qualified and competent martial arts instructor.

Basic Anatomy of the Reverse Crescent Kick

In this chapter, I will attempt to give you a basic understanding of the primary muscular groups and bones in the skeletal system that form the anatomical basis of a Reverse Crescent Kick. I will do this by listing each of the muscle and bones separately and then at the end of each description, I will provide an explanation as to their role in the correct execution of a Back Leg Reverse Crescent Kick. Although the entire body is utilized in the correct execution of a Reverse Crescent Kick, I will only be concentrating on the muscle and skeletal structure of the lower back, hips, legs, and feet.

BONES:

The skeleton of the leg is composed of the femur (thigh bone), tibia and fibula (calf bones), and the patella (kneecap). These bones have three primary sites of articulation; the hip joint, formed by the head of the femur and the acetabulum of the pelvis, the knee joint, formed by the joining of the lower end of the femur, the patella, and the superior end of the tibia and fibula, and the ankle, formed by the articulation between the tibia and the tarsus. The legs are responsible for bearing a great deal of weight and are subjected to intense vertical and lateral stresses, especially at the knee joint. Consequently, the bones of the leg are often cracked or broken, and the knee, hip and ankle joint are particularly susceptible to fracture, strain, sprain, and dislocation.

Each foot is made up of twenty-six bones, which form the ankle, top and bottom of the foot, and toes. These bones are articularly specialized, allowing a wide range of flexibility, while being able to withstand the incredible amounts of stress placed upon them. It is estimated that each stride of an adult places 900 pounds of pressure per square inch on the bottom of the foot. Seven of these bones form the compact arrangement of the ankle, or tarsus, and the heel.

Calcaneus;

The calcaneus bone forms the lower, outer part of the ankle and extends downward to form the heel. It is responsible for bearing much of the immediate stress placed upon the foot during walking and running. **The outside edge of the calcaneus or heel, is the striking implement used when executing a Reverse Crescent Kick.**

Femur;

The femur is the longest bone in the body, and composes the upper leg, or thigh. The upper portion of the femur articulates with the acetabulum, the large circular cavity on each side of the pelvis, to form the ball and socket joint at the hip. The bottom portion of the femur articulates with the tibia and fibula, and the patella (knee cap) to form the knee joint. Each femur directly bears the weight of the entire upper body. **The femur provides support to the lower leg bones (tibia and fibula), at the junction of the knee joint, which lend direct support to the calcaneus bone. The head of the femur also connects to the pelvis.**

Fibula;

The fibula is the smaller of the two bones of the lower leg. It articulates at each

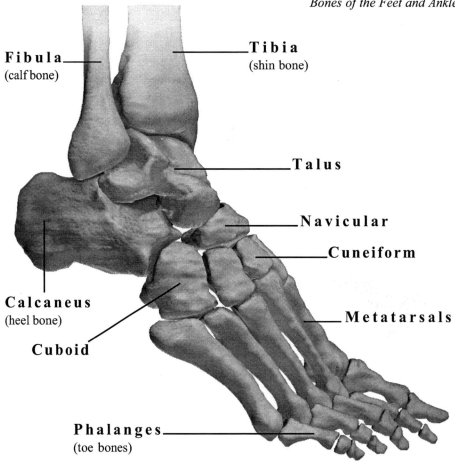

Fibula
(calf bone)

Tibia
(shin bone)

Talus

Navicular

Cuneiform

Calcaneus
(heel bone)

Cuboid

Metatarsals

Phalanges
(toe bones)

end with the parallel tibia, at its upper portion with the femur to form the knee joint, and at its lower portion with the bones of the ankle, or tarsus. The fibula is so named because it serves as a brace for the lower leg. **The fibula along with the tibia, lend direct support to the calcaneus bone, which is the striking implement used in a Reverse Crescent Kick.**

Knee;

The knee is the hinge like joint formed by the lower end of the femur, the upper ends of the tibia and fibula, and the patella (kneecap). The knee is a joint, which is subjected to tremendous lateral stress during normal activity and is guarded by a number of ligaments to help lend it support. Even so, however, the increased stresses placed upon this joint during extreme athletic activity, which require the individual to alter directions rapidly, the knee often bears the brunt of intolerable shearing forces. Such incidences often result in torn ligaments within the knee, which require corrective surgery. Proper technique and attention to detail must be utilized at all times in order to avoid injuring yourself during the execution of any technique. **The knee due to its unique structure and function, can be easily damaged if proper technique is not used during the entire execution of a Reverse Crescent Kick.**

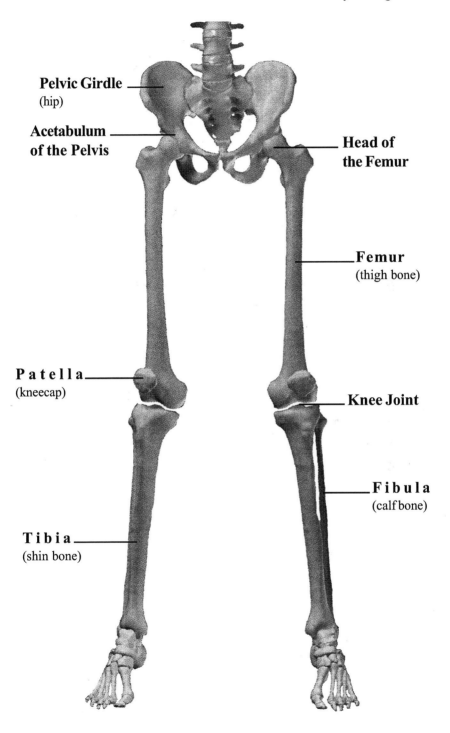

Pelvic Girdle
(hip)

**Acetabulum
of the Pelvis**

**Head of
the Femur**

Femur
(thigh bone)

P a t e l l a
(kneecap)

Knee Joint

F i b u l a
(calf bone)

T i b i a
(shin bone)

Patella;

The patella or kneecap is a small bone of the knee joint, which resembles an inverted teardrop. The patella is connected to the joint by a series of ligaments.

Pelvis;

The pelvis creates the basin of the lower abdominal cavity. It articulates with the sacrum in the back, and thereby connects to the rest of the vertebral column, and also to the legs through the ball and socket joint formed by the two acetabula of the pelvis and the head of each femur. **The pelvis is the connecting link between the actions of the upper and lower body.**

Phalanges;

The bones of the toes are known as phalanges. Each toe has three phalanges, with the exception of the large toe, which has only two. Toes and ankles are the most common self-inflicted injuries when kicking. Keeping your toes back, and out of the way, and your foot tight upon impact will greatly reduce the risk of injury. **The toes provide balance and stability in all activities that involve moving on your feet.**

Tibia;

The tibia is the primary bone of the two in the lower leg. Also called the shinbone, the tibia bears most of the weight. Its upper portion articulates with the parallel fibula, patella and the femur at the knee joint. Its lower portion articulates with the fibula and the talus of the ankle. **The tibia along with the fibula lend direct support to the calcaneus bone, which is the striking implement used in a Reverse Crescent Kick.**

MUSCLES:

The muscles and joints of the legs provide strength and stability for the body. These muscles serve to transmit the weight of the body and provide power for such common activities as walking, running and jumping. They also absorb the cumulative impact of those activities. The leg bones are girded on all sides by sets of powerful muscles that allow the legs to bend (flexion) and straighten (extension) as well as move outward from the body (abduction) and inward (adduction). Some of these muscles are relatively long and participate in more than one type of movement. The thigh consists of the body's largest bone, the femur, which is bound on all sides by sets of powerful muscles.

The calf, ankle and foot are controlled largely by a series of muscles and tendons that function as a single biomechanical unit. These muscles work together to lift or lower the heel for virtually any activity that involves locomotion. All of the parts of the lower leg are interconnected. For example, when you stand on your toes, you can feel the muscles in the back of your calf doing most of the work. Because of its structure, and because it absorbs the impact from activities like running and jumping, the lower leg is subject to more exercise related injuries than any other area of the body. These problems range from bunions and blisters to stress fractures and ankle sprains, the most common sports injury of all.

The feet and toes are essential elements in body movement. They bear and propel the weight of the body during walking and running, and help to maintain balance during changes of body position. The foot can adapt itself to different surfaces and

14

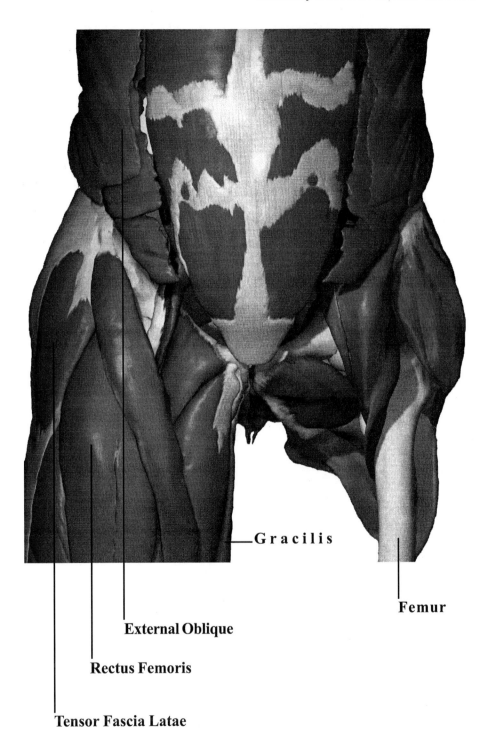

Gracilis

Femur

External Oblique

Rectus Femoris

Tensor Fascia Latae

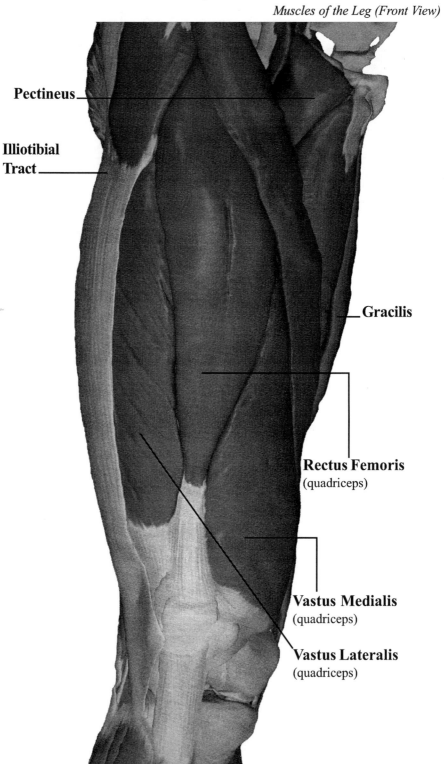

Pectineus

Illiotibial
Tract

Gracilis

Rectus Femoris
(quadriceps)

Vastus Medialis
(quadriceps)

Vastus Lateralis
(quadriceps)

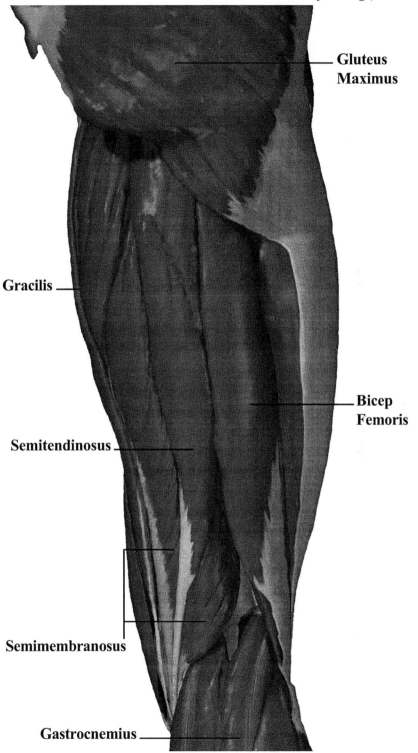

Gluteus
Maximus

Gracilis

Bicep
Femoris

Semitendinosus

Semimembranosus

Gastrocnemius

17

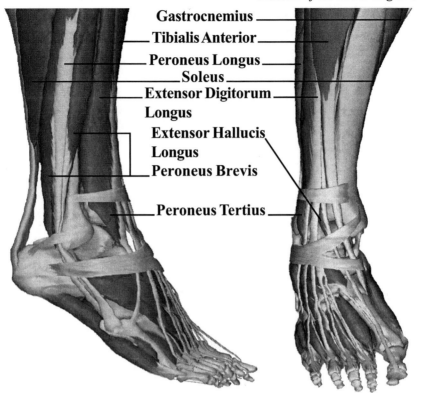

Gastrocnemius
Tibialis Anterior
Peroneus Longus
Soleus
Extensor Digitorum Longus
Extensor Hallucis Longus
Peroneus Brevis
Peroneus Tertius

absorb mechanical shocks as well. Each foot has about thirty-three muscles, some of which are attached to the lower leg.

Bicep Femoris:

The bicep femoris muscle runs from the tuberosity of the ischium down to the back of the head of the fibula. This muscle flexes the lower leg at the knee joint and also abducts or rotates the tibia outward. **This muscle helps extend the leg from the "Follow Through" position to the "End of Arc" position and continuing back to a "Fighting Position." It also acts as a stabilizer and somewhat like a "shock absorber" for the knee itself during impact with the target.**

Extensor Digitorum Longus:

The extensor digitorum longus muscle arises from the tibia and the front of the fibula, and runs down into the foot and the toes. This muscle extends the toes and flexes the foot toward the leg. **This muscle assists in pushing off the floor with your toes during the "Begin Arc" phase of executing a Reverse Crescent Kick. It also flexes the foot toward your knee in order to obtain the proper foot position for a Reverse Crescent Kick.**

Extensor Hallucis Longus:

The extensor hallucis longus muscle lies deep in the lower leg and extends down to the big toe. This muscle extends the big toe and assists in flexing the foot. **As with the extensor digitorum longus, this muscle assists in pushing off the floor** with your big toe during the "Begin Arc" phase of executing a Reverse Crescent Kick. It also flexes the foot toward your knee in order to obtain the proper foot position for a Reverse Crescent Kick.

External Oblique:

The external oblique muscle runs along the side of the torso and partially on the front from the lower ribs to the rectus, the pubis bone, and iliac crest of the hip. This muscle assists the rectus abdominus muscle in flexing the spine when the trunk twists or turns. **This muscle assists with the flexing of the spine and abdomen when executing a Reverse Crescent Kick.**

Flexor Digitorum Longus:

The flexor digitorum longus muscle runs deep in the lower leg from the middle of the tibia to underneath the foot to the toes. This muscle assists to flex the toes during the final push off in walking or running. **As with the extensor digitorum longus and the extensor hallucis longus, this muscle assists in pushing off the floor with your toes during the "Begin Arc" phase of executing a Reverse Crescent Kick.**

Gastrocnemius:

The gastrocnemius muscle runs from the back of the knee to the ankle to form the calf muscle. This muscle propels the body when walking, running or jumping. It raises the heel, which lifts the body. It also assists, though minimally, in flexing the knee joint. **This muscle assists the bicep femoris in rasing the heel of your foot off the ground when you begin to initiate a Reverse Crescent Kick.**

Gemelli:

The gemelli are two small muscles of the hip. The muscles arise from the spine and insert into the upper edge of the thighbone. These muscles help rotate the thigh. **This muscle helps rotate the thigh when you first begin to initiate a Reverse Crescent Kick by raising your leg up from the "Begin Arc" position to the "Peak of Arc" position.**

Gluteus Maximus:

We sit on the largest and most powerful muscle in our body, the gluteus maximus. This muscle powerfully extends the thigh at the hip joint and moves it away from the body, as when walking or running. **This muscle helps raise the leg up to the "Peak of Arc" position, as well as, extending the leg from the "Follow Through" position back down to a "Fighting Position." Proper utilization of this muscle will greatly increase the power in your Reverse Crescent Kick.**

Gluteus Medius:

The gluteus medius runs from the outer portion of the pelvis, up to the crest of the pelvis. The gluteus medius is partially covered by the gluteus maximus. It moves the thigh outward and rotates it, as when walking or running. It keeps the torso upright during walking when one foot is touching the ground and the other is not. **This muscle assists in raising the leg up to the "Peak of Arc" position.**

Gracilis:

The gracilis muscle lies on the inside of the femur and begins at the pubic arch and runs down towards the inside of the tibia or shinbone. This muscle brings the knee up and pulls it across the front, toward the middle of the body. It also assists in rotation of the leg. **This is the primary muscle utilized when raising the thigh up towards the abdomen from the "Begin Arc" position to the "Peak of Arc" position.**

Iliopsoas:

The iliopsoas runs from deep in the back of the abdomen towards its insertion on the back of the femur. This muscle flexes the hip and assists in abduction and outward rotation of the hip. **This muscle assists in flexing the thigh towards the abdomen and assists in raising the leg up to the "Peak of Arc" position.**

Iliotibial Tract:

The iliotibial tract begins at the upper edge of the femur and ends where it inserts into the condyle of the tibia. It acts almost like a ligament, by helping mainly to stabilize the knee joint, but also acts in flexing (bending) and extending (straightening) the knee. **This muscle assists in straightening and stabilizing the knee during the execution of a Reverse Crescent Kick.**

Pectineus:

The pectineus muscle lies on the front of the upper and middle part of the thigh. This muscle flexes and moves the thigh towards the body and rotates it towards the center. **This muscle helps flex the hip creating added force (not speed) to the Reverse Crescent Kick. It also assists with bringing the kicking leg back down from the "Follow Through" position to the "End of Arc" position and continuing back to a "Fighting Position."**

Peroneus Brevis:

The peroneus brevis muscle runs along the outside of the lower half of the fibula or lower leg. This muscle works with the peroneus longus to extend the foot. **This muscle helps extend the foot as when pushing off the floor to move into the "Begin Arc" position.**

Peroneus Longus:

The peroneus longus muscle runs along the upper part of the outside of the fibula or lower leg. This muscle works with the peroneus brevis to extend the foot. **This muscle, along with the peroneus brevis, helps extend the foot as when pushing off the floor to move into the "Begin Arc" position.**

Peroneus Tertius:

The peroneus tertius runs from the lower third of the fibula downward and slightly forward, across the ankle and inserts into the little toe. This muscle provides dorsiflexion and eversion of the foot. **This muscle helps the foot maintain its proper position in order to execute a Reverse Crescent Kick.**

Plantaris:

The plantaris muscle runs from the lower end of the femur down to a small area on the bottom of the calcaneus or heel bone. This muscle works with the gastrocnemius to extend the ankle if the foot is free, and bend the knee if the foot is fixed, as when walking. **This muscle helps extend the foot as when pushing off the floor to move into the "Begin Arc" position.**

Popliteal Region:

The popliteal muscle starts from the femur and the ligament behind the knee joint and extends down to the shaft of the tibia or shinbone. This muscle assists in rotating the tibia and is used when bending the knee. **This muscle is used to slightly bend the knee on the kicking leg prior to impact.**

Quadriceps:

The quadriceps consists of four separate muscles. The rectus femoris, which runs from the ilium or hipbone down to the knee. This muscle flexes the hip joint and helps with hip joint abduction. The vastus lateralis is located halfway down the outside of the thigh, this muscle extends the knee, but it needs the vastus medialis in order to give a straight pull to the knee. The vastus intermedius lies between the vastus medialis and the vastus lateralis, and beneath the rectus femoris. This muscle extends the knee with its pull directly upward on the patella. And finally the vastus medialis, which is located above the knee, on the top of the thigh. This muscle extends the knee with the assistance of the vastus lateralis. These muscles cover the front and sides of the femur or thigh, and work together as a primary extensor of the knee. The rectus femoris muscle extends the leg at the knee joint and flexes the thigh at the hip joint. **The rectus femoris primarily flexes the thigh towards the abdomen and assists in raising the leg up to the "Peak of Arc" position. All four-quadriceps muscles work together to straighten the knee when executing a Reverse Crescent Kick.**

Semimembranosus:

The semimembranosus muscle begins in the tuberosity of the ischium or underneath and back of the pelvis, and runs two-thirds of the way down the back of the thigh to the outer condyle of the femur or upper leg, just above the knee. This muscle extends the thigh and assists with the inward rotation of the hip joint. It also provides flexion and inward rotation for the knee. **This muscle along with the semitendinosus assists in extending the thigh from the "Follow Through" position to the "End of Arc" position and continuing back to a "Fighting Position."**

Semitendinosus:

The semitendinosus muscle begins in the ischium or bottom and back of the pelvis, and runs two-thirds of the way down the middle of the back of the thigh. It is considered one of the hamstring muscles. This muscle flexes the lower leg and extends the thigh at the hip joint. It also provides flexion and inward rotation for the knee. **This muscle along with the semimembranosus assists in extending the thigh from the "Follow Through" position to the "End of Arc" position and continuing back to a "Fighting Position."**

Soleus:

The soleus muscle is located on the back of the lower leg and runs from the upper part of the fibula down to the middle portion of the calcaneus or heel bone. This muscle is used to point the foot or raise the heel, which lifts the body. **This muscle raises the heel off the floor when you begin to initiate a Reverse Crescent Kick.**

Tensor Fascia Latae:

The tensor fascia latae muscle is located on the outer front corner of the ilium or hipbone. It connects the ilium to the tissues of the outer thigh. This muscle flexes, abducts, and medially rotates the thigh. **This muscle assists in the raising of the leg up to the "Peak of Arc" position.**

Tibialis Anterior:

The tibialis anterior muscle sits on the front of the tibia, and originates from the outside of the tibia below the knee and runs down into the foot. This muscle controls the descent of the foot during walking after the heel strikes the ground. **This muscle assists in keeping your foot in the proper position in order to execute a Reverse Crescent Kick.**

Tibialis Posterior:

The tibialis posterior muscle originates from the back of the tibia, behind the knee, and runs down into the foot. This muscle flexes the foot and, working with the tibialis anterior, turns the sole of the foot inward. It is the strongest support for the arch of the foot. **This muscle is responsible for adding "spring" to your foot when stepping or running.**

Note: Take a real close physical and philosophical look at the illustration presented above, and then compare it to the kick that is explained in great detail in this book. Now write down in detail, what this illustration represent to you.

Warm Up and Stretching

Although stretching is perhaps the single greatest activity that you can perform to improve your kicking (other than utilizing proper technique), I am not going to go into great detail on the types of stretches to perform. Instead, I will try and give you a firm understanding on the do's and don'ts of proper stretching. So without further delay, let's get started.

It is a well-known fact that active people tend to lead fuller more productive lives due to better health. Their endurance and stamina are greater not only during exercise, but also during normal everyday activities; such as climbing stairs, walking, doing normal household chores, etc. Medical research has shown us over the years, that poor health is directly related to our increasingly sedentary life-style.

Research has also shown us that exercise, done at any age, retards the aging factor and allows our bodies to become healthier and more resistant to disease. It is obvious that as we become less active, we begin to lose not only our physical strength, but our mental strength as well. Therefore, our ability to utilize our bodies potential is greatly diminished. However, we can regain that potential and more through a correct and consistent stretching and training program.

Without a daily regiment of stretching and physical conditioning, our bodies become atrophied and weak with stored up tension, both physical and mental. Let's face it, regardless of how out of shape you are from lack of physical activity and poor eating habits, your body's potential to recover from this mistreatment, and in fact flourish to new levels of health and increased physical abilities, is nothing short of phenomenal.

What does stretching do for your body? Well primarily, it keeps your muscles and connective tissue flexible and more resilient to injury. It also prepares your body for more vigorous activity. This is similar to starting your automobiles engine in cold weather and allowing it to idle for several minutes before driving. This idling period allows the engine of your car to warm up before the more strenuous demands of driving are placed upon it. Stretching is the idling period for your body. Stretching is essential to any martial art or combat sport, if you wish to perform at your optimum level, whether that is in the dojo, on the street, or in competition. Stretching in and of itself is easy to do, when performed correctly and consistently, and should take you between 25 to 35 minutes depending upon your level of fitness.

However, when performed incorrectly, it can actually cause injuries and impede your progress. It is for this reason that I recommend that you utilize your head when stretching and take your time. Perform the stretches correctly and slowly for the best results. Stretch at your own pace, not someone else's.

A regular program of correct stretching will help you avoid injuries and will allow you to perform to the best of your abilities. Stretching, when performed correctly, should not be painful. You should be able to feel the stretch, as it is performed in a slow relaxing manner. Your body should not be tense nor should you force your body when stretching. Stretching should be a relaxing and warming up process, which takes place before performing a strenuous exercise.

Do Not make stretching a strenuous exercise. Your goal to achieve when stretching should be to reduce tension in the muscles, which will allow you to stretch even further. This will result in a greatly improved level of flexibility. For the best results, stretch before and after participating in any strenuous activity, in addition to a daily stretching routine. A good stretching program can be adjusted to suit the needs of the individual. Certain characteristics to keep in mind when developing a stretching program are; type of activity involved in, personal goals, body type, current level of flexibility, and most important, your current physical condition.

Anyone who actively participates in a correct stretching program on a regular basis can become more flexible and improve their overall physical conditioning. You don't have to be able to perform the splits or be the reincarnation of Bruce Lee in order to gain flexibility, but you do have to have the desire and the willingness to train on a daily basis, and perhaps more importantly, you must learn to be patient with yourself.

Do's and Don'ts of Stretching:

Do's:
1. Wear loose fitting, yet comfortable clothing that will not impede movement and will keep your body warm in cold or inclement weather.
2. Perform a light exercise to get your body warmed up such as jumping rope, running in place, etc.
3. Hold each stretch for 10 to 30 seconds. Relax. Then go a little farther into your stretch and hold for another 10 to 30 seconds.
4. Keep your breathing slow and under control.
5. Keep track of the time during each stretch by slowly counting to yourself.
6. When your are performing the stretch correctly, you should feel a mild tension in the muscles. It should not be painful.
7. Take your time when stretching.
8. Stretch every day for 25 to 35 minutes.
9. Pay attention to your body and what it tells you.

Don'ts:
1. Bounce up and down while stretching.
2. Over stretch to where it becomes painful.
3. Hold your breath while stretching.

Perhaps the greatest example of what a daily program of stretching can do for you is brought to us from the animal kingdom. The most dangerous and skillful hunters are without a doubt the cats. From the regal "king of the beasts" on the plains of Africa, to our own domestic house cats. No other animal displays such a tremendous combination of flexibility, agility, and strength as the cat. Watch them and learn. Remember that Rome wasn't built in a day, and neither shall you.

Basic Principles of Movement
for the Back Leg Reverse Crescent Kick

In this chapter, I will give you a basic understanding of the kicking principles involved in the correct execution of a Reverse Crescent Kick. Although a lot of these principles are the same for the other primary kicks and their variations, there are others that are exclusive only to the Back Leg Reverse Crescent Kick and its variations. Study each one of these in detail until you know them inside and out. The more you know about a kick, the better you will be able to execute it.

Striking Implement:

The striking implement utilized in executing any Reverse Crescent Kick, is the outside edge of the heel or calcaneus bone. This bone extends down from the ankle to form the heel. When a Reverse Crescent Kick is properly executed, with the outside edge of the heel as the striking implement, the bones and muscles of the ankle, lower leg, upper leg, and hip provide additional support upon impact with the target. As you can see, in the photographs on the right, hitting with the upper knife edge of the foot or the outside of the ankle, would result in little more than a push or hard slap, when executing a Reverse Crescent Kick.

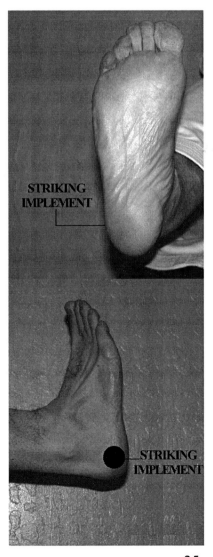

STRIKING IMPLEMENT

STRIKING IMPLEMENT

Remember, the idea is not to inflict damage upon yourself, but rather to your opponent when executing a Reverse Crescent Kick. Therefore, you must constantly be aware of your foot position and proper striking surface every time you kick, even if you are only kicking air.

One way to produce a greater amount of force is to utilize a smaller surface area when striking your intended target. Let's say for the sake of argument that you can deliver a total of 100 lbs. of force to your target, and that the surface area of your heel is equal to 2 square inches. If you strike the target correctly with your heel, you will be able to deliver 50 lbs. of pressure per square inch. If however you strike the target incorrectly with your entire foot or leg, which has a surface area of say 20 square inches, then you would be striking your target with 5 lbs. of pressure per square inch. Do you see what the difference is between striking with the correct surface area of the foot and the incorrect surface area? Not quite sure, let me put it to you another way. Try hammering a nail into a piece of wood using the pointed end of the nail to make contact with the board first, and then hammering on the head of the nail. Then take another nail and lay it on its side and try hammering it into the wood?

Now do you see the relevancy of striking with the correct surface area? Although the amount of force exerted against your opponent in both cases are equal, the pressure exerted upon the target struck correctly with the heel is five times greater than if you used the entire surface area of your foot. When you strike the intended target with to large a surface area, you are dissipating the force over a wider surface area resulting in a push or surface strike rather than a penetrating impact. This greatly reduces the effectiveness of your kick.

Target Areas:

I define the target area as, the general location of a vital or vulnerable point on the human body. For the greatest effectiveness with the Reverse Crescent Kick in combat, you want to strike a particular vital or vulnerable point every time you strike your opponent. This will most likely deter any continued attack from your opponent by causing pain and/or injury. However, this is not always possible as very few individuals are going to stand there and let you hit them. They are going to be moving, blocking, dodging and perhaps more importantly trying to hit you back. Therefore, you want to be able to strike your opponent the most effective and efficient way that you can.

One component of that is a thorough knowledge of the vital or vulnerable points of the human body. Not only is this knowledge important to inflict damage upon your opponent (only when absolutely necessary), but also to enable you to avoid such damage being inflicted upon yourself. I am not going to discuss in detail the vital or vulnerable points in this book. However, I am going to list the general target areas and the vital or vulnerable points that lie within those areas that you will want to strike with a Reverse Crescent Kick. For more detailed information on vital or vulnerable points, please refer to the recommended reading section at the back of this book.

The effects of striking each vital or vulnerable point vary drastically depending on the accuracy, direction, speed, and power utilized when striking them. Another factor that has to be taken into consideration is the human factor. Each individual is vastly different from the next and each person is going to react differently when struck. Some people may go down from the lightest of blows, while others will merely shake off your strongest blows and keep coming at you. Which is a very good reason why you should have a thorough understanding of vital or vulnerable points.

Be prepared for any and all eventualities. Because serious injury or even death may result from forceful blows to these target areas, you must exercise extreme caution when practicing with a partner, and you should never actually strike any of these areas with even the lightest blows in practice. If you are called upon to strike these areas in self-defense, you should only use full force to save one's life. Along

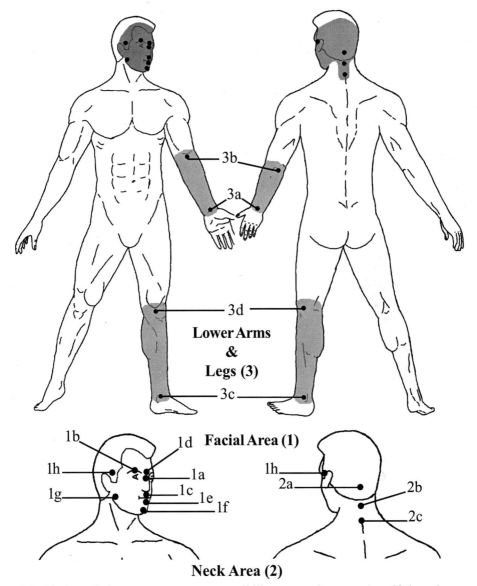

Lower Arms & Legs (3)

Facial Area (1)

Neck Area (2)

with this knowledge comes great responsibility, not only to one's self, but also to those around you. **Never Use Excessive Force!**

1. **Facial Area:** This target area encompasses the nose (1a), orbital bones (1b), the philtrum (1c), glabella (1d), mouth (1e), point of chin (1f), the jaw (1g), and the temple (1h).

2. **Neck Area:** This target area encompasses the occipital bone (2a), 3rd intervertebral space (2b), and the spine (2c).

3. **Lower Arms & Legs:** These target areas are the wrists (3a), elbows (3b), ankles (3c), and the knees (3d).

Each one of these vital or vulnerable points can be struck separately utilizing the Reverse Crescent Kick.

Stability:

For the purpose of the material presented in this book, stability is defined as, "A person's ability to stand upon any given surface in a controlled and capable manner." For example you would have an easier time executing a kick on a hard flat surface such as cement or pavement, than you would if you were standing on gravel or ice. Sometimes it is necessary to create a very stable position or stance, such as when delivering a powerful kick.

Other times it is important to be in an unstable position, such as moving quickly in order to avoid being hit. Therefore a thorough understanding of the following principles will give you the ability to apply them on a daily basis, whether it be in practice, self-defense, or in competition. Several different factors contribute to one's stability such as your weight, height, center of gravity, equilibrium or balance, and your base of support. Let's take a look at each one of these factors.

Weight:

With all other factors being equal, a heavier person is generally speaking more stable than a lighter person. Consequently, a heavier person such as World Heavyweight Boxing Champion George Foreman would be harder to push off balance than a lighter person such as World Boxing Champion Oscar De LaHoya. It also stands to reason that Foreman is able to punch harder from his heavier and more solid position than De LaHoya is from his lighter and less solid position.

However, no one would argue the fact that De LaHoya, being a lighter weight fighter, has the advantage of being able to move and change direction quicker than the heavier Foreman. This is of course taking into consideration that all other factors involved are equal. I have seen some very big men that could move a lot faster and a lot smoother than their smaller counterparts.

Height and Center of Gravity:

Your center of gravity is defined as being located approximately 2 to 3 inches below your belly button and in the center of your body when standing perfectly straight with correct posture, and your feet flat on the floor. This of course varies from person to person and also upon their general body type. Women tend to have a lower center of gravity than men, and individuals with heavier legs have a lower center of gravity than someone with lighter legs. The closer one's center of gravity is to the ground or base of support, the greater their increase in stability.

You can easily change your center of gravity by bending your knees and squatting down to lower it, or by standing on your toes to raise it. You can even move your center of gravity outside your body by bending over at the waist and touching your toes. Generally speaking, the taller you are the less stability you have, while the shorter you are the more stability you have. Ask yourself this question, which has more stability the giraffe or the hippopotamus?

Equilibrium:

Equilibrium is defined as a state of balance between opposing forces. A prime example of equilibrium is a figure skaters ability to stand upon the toes of their skates while spinning their entire body into a tightly controlled blur of motion and then stopping without any outwards signs of loss of balance or equilibrium. For equilibrium to exist, your center of gravity must be centered over your base of support throughout the entire sequence of events involved when executing a Crescent Kick, or any other athletic endeavor. Failure to maintain equilibrium will result in a loss of balance, and can result in a slight case of disorientation. Either of which could prove disastrous in a self-defense or tournament situation.

Base of Support:

Your base of support is described as the area of the feet upon which the weight of your body is supported, along with the space between your feet. For example,

(A) if you were standing flat footed with both feet on the ground and directly beneath your shoulders, your base of support would not only include both feet, but also the space between them.

(B) If you were standing on the toes of both feet, your base of support would include the surface area of your feet that are in direct contact with the ground and the space between them.

And

(C) if you were balancing on the ball of one foot, your base of support would be the surface area covered by the ball of your base foot.

Generally speaking, the greater the surface area of your feet that is in direct contact with the ground, and the wider the stance, the greater your base of support.

Therefore, after taking all of these factors into consideration, it stands to reason that the heavier, shorter individual is more stable during the execution of a punch when both feet are on the ground, than the lighter taller individual is when executing a kick and balancing on one leg. Does this mean that you are better off punching than kicking? Of course not, it simply means that the skills needed to kick effectively take a lot more time, effort, and attention to detail than those skills needed to punch effectively.

This is one of the reasons why so many people tend to neglect their kicking skills in favor of the easier learned punching and grappling skills. Your stance when fighting should be unstable in that you should not be set in one position, you should be constantly moving in order to avoid an attack while positioning yourself to effectively attack your opponent.

If your stance is too wide, you will sacrifice mobility as well as telegraphing any kick that you may attempt. This in effect makes you a sitting duck. If your stance is too short, you will have lost balance and stability. The ideal stance is to keep your feet shoulder width apart in length and about 4 to 8 inches apart in width.

Balance:

Although the previous section on stability also included information on equilibrium or balance, this section is devoted to balance as it applies to the execution of a kick. If you do not have good balance when kicking, not only is your kick going to be ineffective, but you may have put yourself in a dangerous situation by overextending your kicking leg, losing your balance all together, and possibly even falling to the ground. In order to prevent this, you must follow these few simple points when executing your kick.

1. Your center of gravity must be centrally located over your base foot throughout the entire kicking sequence from start to finish.

2. In order to execute your kick, you are going to pivot on the ball of your base foot. However, the entire base foot must be in direct contact with the ground at the moment of impact, with your center of gravity in the middle of the foot, not over the ball, heel, inner or outer edge of the foot. After the initial contact is made, you will continue with the "Follow Through" and then return the kicking foot to the starting position by once again pivoting on the ball of the base foot. You should never make contact with your target while balancing on the ball of your base foot. This incorrect technique is not only unstable, but it also causes a dramatic decrease in the effectiveness of the kick.

3. The position of your base foot is directly related to the effectiveness of maintaining your balance when kicking. For example the inside edge of your base foot is facing directly toward your opponent during the "Impact" phase of a Reverse Crescent Kick. However, in most cases, your big toe will be slightly closer to your opponent than your heel. Try performing the Reverse Crescent Kick with the toes of your base foot pointed at your opponent; now try it with the heel pointed at your opponent. Did they work? How does your knee and hips feel?

4. And finally, don't forget the importance of that area of the body above your waist. I always find it amazing how many people forget about how important proper upper body position is to achieving and maintaining balance when kicking. Keep your head up and looking at your opponent, keep your back straight, and stop moving your arms around like a bird flapping its wings.

You'll be surprised at how much your kicks have improved by simply paying attention to these few things.

Alignment:

Your entire body should be aligned properly at the moment of impact in order to generate the maximum amount of power into the delivery of your kick upon its target. The proper body alignment at the moment of impact for the Reverse Crescent Kick is as follows. The kicking foot is perpendicular to the ground, and the outside edge of the heel should be the only part of the foot in contact with the target. The toes should be pulled back towards your knee and pointed straight up in the air in a vertical position. This not only exposes the outside edge of the heel for better contact, but it also tightens the ankle.

The lower leg, knee, and upper leg should all be in a straight line and supporting one another in order to increase the overall effectiveness of the kick. The kicking leg hip, shoulder, back, and the head should all be in a straight line with the heel. The inside edge of the base leg foot is facing almost directly toward your opponent and the supporting base leg is straight. This will have the effect of putting your entire body behind the kick, where the culmination of muscular speed, strength and proper technique combine to deliver the generated force into your target along a straight line of trajectory.

Sequence of Movement:

What this means is that the correct sequence of movements from the beginning stages of the kick, to the impact and subsequent follow through, should be followed in one smooth continuous motion in order to achieve the maximum effectiveness out of your kick. In order to do this however, you must first work upon each individual section of the kick until you can effectively flow from one to the other without any noticeable pauses or breaks between them. Even though the Reverse Crescent Kick should be performed in one fluid motion, there are three distinct and separate sections to this kick. The first is the delivery of the kick to the "Peak of Arc," the second is the straight and level "Path of Trajectory," which begins with the "Peak of Arc" through "Impact" and continues to the "Follow Through" position. The third is the recovery after delivering the kick. Combine the three, but keep them separate.

Accuracy:

No matter how perfectly you execute your Reverse Crescent Kick, it isn't going to do you one ounce of good unless you can hit your intended target. Imagine going out to war and being equipped with the biggest most powerful rifle you can get, and then not being able to hit your target. Now combine that with the fact that the guy you are fighting against is equipped with a .22 caliber rifle and the ability to hit a dime at 100 yards. Who do you think is going to survive that encounter? There are several factors involved in obtaining accurate kicks such as eye contact, proper technique, muscular control or coordination, breath control, conditioning, and most importantly, proper practice.

Eye Contact:

Your eyes should remain in constant contact with your opponent at all times. The focus of your attention should be like a flashlight on your opponent's chest, while your peripheral vision encompasses everything else from his head to his hands and down to his feet. Be careful not to focus your eyes like a laser beam on one single point, this can cause a delayed reaction time to incoming attacks and can also telegraph your intentions to your opponent.

Practice Proper Technique:

The ability to kick proficiently is not instinctive, it is a learned activity that takes years of study and constant practice to perfect. I cannot stress this simple fact enough, "Pay Attention To Detail and Practice!" The kicks presented in this book have been explained in precise detail so that you can learn the proper technique for executing them as efficiently and as accurately as possible. Practice and study the material in this book until it becomes second nature.

Muscular Control or Coordination:

This is the ability to control ones own body during physical activities such as kicking. This is not an easy skill to learn, and it takes a considerable amount of practice in order to utilize it effectively. The best method that I know of to improve your muscular control for kicking, is to perform the entire kicking sequence in slow motion until the point of impact, at which point you hold that position for approximately five seconds tensing your entire body during that time. After the five seconds are over, relax the entire body and slowly continue with the "Follow Through" returning to your original starting position. This should be performed at least 10 times prior to and at the end of every kicking session. Another variation of this technique is to tense all of your muscles during the entire time you are performing this exercise. This is called Dynamic Tension training and is very effective.

Breathing:

You should never hold your breath when fighting. Breathing should be done normally by inhaling through your nose and exhaling through your mouth. Remember to keep your mouth closed when fighting. Don't open it or you may get a broken jaw for your trouble. At the exact moment that you make impact with your target, you will exhale sharply, and tighten your entire body, this will add power to your kick.

Conditioning:

Physical conditioning is an absolute must if you want to perform these kicks to the best of your abilities. The better condition that you are in, the more that you will be able to do for a longer period of time before becoming fatigued. The harder you train, the easier it will become.

Strength:

Strength is the amount of muscular force that you can apply at any given time to a particular target. Don't confuse strength with power. Speed and strength are two sides of the same coin which when combined together create power. Pivoting of the hips and the turning of the body are two methods of applying strength to a kick with minimal muscular effort. I am sure you have heard of a boxer who uses only his arms when he punches rather than utilizing his entire body. The same is also true of kicking, in that the majority of individuals kick only with their legs, rather than with their entire body.

Leg strength alone does not give any real strength to the kick. Granted there is some strength present, however, it is minimal compared to the strength that can be delivered if the entire body is utilized in the execution of the kick. The positioning of your head, arms, hands, and upper body are also instrumental in increasing the strength of your kick.

Speed:

The only drawbacks to kicking are that although the leg is longer than the arm, it is relatively slower, and if you don't practice your kicking skills regularly they tend to deteriorate and lose their speed. Speed and strength are two side of the same coin, which when combined together creates power. To best explain this principle I like to use the analogy of a Lamborghini and a bulldozer.

Which one of the two is faster yet not very forceful? Which one is more forceful yet slower? Obviously the Lamborghini is faster and the bulldozer is more forceful. Yet if both of these vehicles started at the same time from one mile away and they both drove as fast as they could until they hit a brick wall at the end of that mile, which one would hit first, and second? And what would happen to them? Obviously the Lamborghini traveling in excess of 200 plus miles per hour would strike the wall long before the much slower bulldozer. However, when it hit the wall it would totally destroy the car and I am sure would cause some minor damage to the wall.

The bulldozer on the other hand, would take a considerably longer amount of time to cover that distance in order to reach the wall, however, once it reached the wall, its greater strength would easily go through it. My whole point being that your body should be like the blinding speed of the Lamborghini as your foot travels to reach its target. However, at the moment of impact, your foot and entire body should transform itself instantaneously from the blinding speed of the Lamborghini into the wall-crushing strength of the bulldozer.

Immediately after impact, your entire body will return to the blinding speed of the Lamborghini in order to facilitate a faster "Follow Through" and return to the starting position. A relaxed muscle is faster, while a tense or contracted muscle is slower yet stronger. Utilize this to your best advantage when executing these kicks.

Distance and Timing:

If the opponent is too far away, how are you going to hit him? If you execute a kick too slow or too fast, and your opponent moves, how are you going to hit him? If you attempt to execute a kick and your opponent is too close to you and jams the kick, how are your going to hit him? These are just a few of the problems that can be solved by creating the proper distance between you and your opponent and the utilization of proper timing. You cannot leave it up to chance or fate to create the perfect kicking distance between you and your opponent, you have to control the distance, and therefore the fight. Don't allow your opponent that opportunity.

Impact:

Impact is the culmination of all of the other principles and techniques performed correctly, in order to generate the maximum amount of force, and to transfer that power into your opponent at the precise moment of impact. If any one technique or principle is neglected, or applied improperly, then you will not be able to produce the maximum amount of force upon impact that you are capable of.

Follow Through:

Proper "Follow Through" of the foot and leg after kicking is perhaps one of the most important movements you can make during the kicking sequence. To begin with, the faster your follow through is after striking your target, the more effective your kick is going to be. This is primarily due to the transfer of energy that is being delivered from your entire body through your leg and foot into the intended target at the moment of impact. The longer your striking implement is in contact with its target, the more energy that is reflected back into you rather than being transferred into the target.

Secondly, the longer you have your foot in the air, the longer it is going to take you to follow up with another technique. It also allows your opponent the opportunity to grab your foot or leg and put you in a world of hurt. Unlike the movies where an actor can kick ten opponents all at once and never put his foot back on the ground, you should never attempt such a foolish stunt. Multiple kicks with one leg in the air can be effective, but only after years and years of devoted practice, and a cooperative opponent. As a general rule-of-thumb, as fast as your kick leaves the ground, it should be just as fast if not faster getting back down on the ground.

Visualization:

"Any sport is 95 percent mental, and anyone who tells you differently, doesn't know what he's talking about," Joe Fields, center for the New York Jets.

"Mind is everything, muscles are pieces of rubber," Paavo Nurmi, Olympic Gold Medallist.

Like I stated before, your mind controls your body. Therefore, you have to believe in yourself and your abilities, if you ever want to become more proficient than what you currently are. There are three separate and unique times that one should utilize visualization as an effective training tool. They are; before, during, and after every practice.

Before:

When you use visualization before practice you want to envision yourself performing the fastest, most powerful, most technically perfect kick you have ever done. Do not envision anything other than perfection. If you see yourself making mistakes or performing a kick poorly, then you will. If you see yourself doing your best then you will do your best. This is also referred to as positive thinking. It works, so use it. This should take anywhere from 5 to 15 minutes.

During:

As you are performing the kick, envision an imaginary target in front of you that you want to kick. Aim your kick to hit a certain target. Be aware of your body movement and position throughout the entire kicking sequence. Imagine your target being totally devastated by your kick. Concentrate!

After:

Use this time to reflect upon your workout and how well you did. Envision yourself doing even better the next time you practice. Answer this question, "If you don't believe in you, who will?"

Back Leg Reverse Crescent Kick

The Back Leg Reverse Crescent Kick is one of the ten primary kicks associated with Karate and/or Tae Kwon Do. Although it goes by many different names, the Back Leg Reverse Crescent Kick, when performed properly, is one of the easiest kicks to learn in the martial artist's arsenal. This section will go into minute detail over all areas and phases of the Back Leg Reverse Crescent Kick. Once this primary kick is mastered, all of the other variations of this primary kick will fall into place. Without any further ado, let's get started.

Fighting Stance:

Your fighting stance should be approximately shoulder width apart (1a) with the toes of your front or lead foot pointed directly at your opponent. The heel of your lead foot should be in a direct line (1b) with the heel of your rear foot. This allows for you to shift your weight onto your base leg (without telegraphing it), which allows you the opportunity to initiate a faster kick. Remember that the foot positions in this stance will actually change after you become comfortable executing this kick. At that time your feet will still be approximately shoulder width apart in length, however the heels will be about 4 to 8 inches apart, rather than in a straight line with one another.

The toes of your back or rear foot (1b) should be pointed away from your body at a 45-degree angle. For example, if your right foot were in the rear position, then the toes of that foot would be pointed to the right at a 45-degree angle. If the left foot were in the rear position, then the toes of your left foot would be pointed to the left at a 45-degree angle.

Your weight should be distributed over the balls of both feet and not over the entire surface are of the feet. This way your mobility is increased and you will be able to initiate a faster more effective Reverse Crescent Kick. The weight distribution over your feet should be approximately 55% over the lead leg and 45% over the rear leg. This also allows for faster movement when kicking or when evading your opponent's attack.

Your knees (2) should be slightly but not noticeably bent. The lead leg knee should be slightly bent over the lead leg foot in the direction of the toes. The same also holds true for the rear knee in the fact that it too should be slightly bent over the rear foot in the direction of the rear toes. The bending of the knees contributes to faster movement with the legs as they are not locked straight or rigid and have better mobility when slightly bent rather than straight.

Your body (3) is facing at a 45-degree angle to your opponent. This presents a smaller target area facing toward your opponent. It also allows you better mobility moving forward toward your opponent, or backward away from your opponent. Additionally, it allows you quicker access to offset your opponent by moving in the direction your body is facing.

Your hands (4a) and elbows (4b), should be held up like a boxer's, that is with the lead hand held up at head level and away from your face about 8 to 12 inches (toward your opponent). Your lead elbow should be tucked in along your side in order to protect your ribs and stomach area. Your rear hand is held up alongside your cheek or neck, with the palm of that hand facing toward your cheek. Your rear elbow is also tucked in along your side in order to protect your ribs and stomach area.

Your back (5) should be straight but not rigid and your lead shoulder should be raised up slightly in order to protect your chin.

Your head (6) is facing toward your opponent with the chin tucked down behind your upraised lead shoulder.

Your eyes (7) should focus like a flashlight on your opponent's chest to center your vision. At the same time, allow your peripheral vision to scan the rest of your opponent's body and therefore any movements he will make. A word of caution, **<u>do not</u>** become fixated on a particular spot or point of focus on your opponent. This becomes more of a hindrance than an asset when fighting.

Additionally, you should **never** take your eyes off your opponent for any reason. This mistake is quite common when first learning how to perform this kick. Always make your point of focus your opponent's chest in order to maintain eye contact with your opponent. Remember the old saying, "Look before you leap?"

Fighting Position Foot Position
(Beginning)

Fighting Position Foot Position
(Advanced)

Note: To better understand the visual aspects of a Back Leg Reverse Crescent Kick, imagine that you are standing in front of, and looking at, the clock image which is shown on the right. The center point of the clock represents your hips. Your base leg is represented by the hour hand, while the minute hand represents your kicking leg. In the advanced "Fighting Position," your kicking leg is just slightly past the 6 o'clock position.

Front View

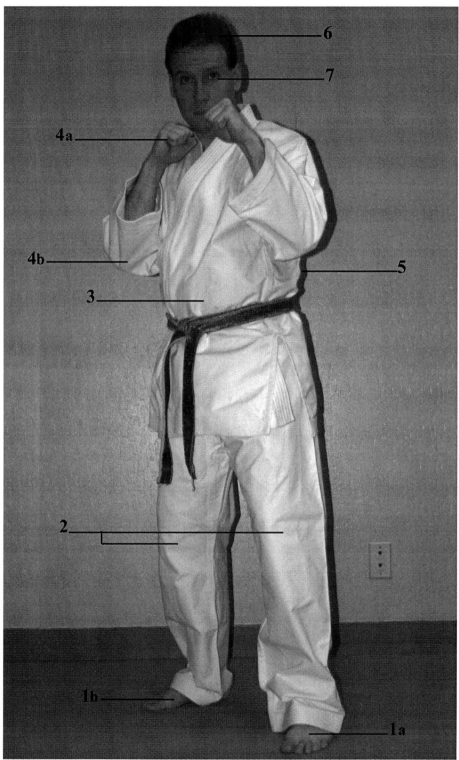

Fighting Position Front View

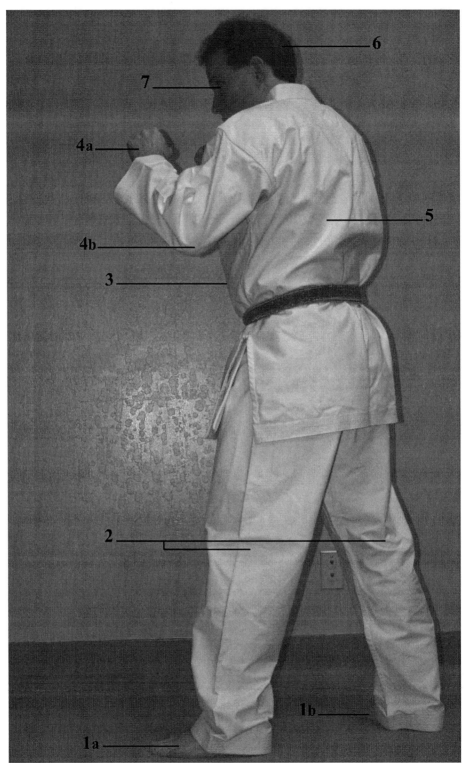

Fighting Position Side View

Begin Arc:

Shifting your weight onto your base leg foot (8), while simultaneously utilizing the toes of your kicking foot (11), push off the floor while pivoting approximately 45-degrees counterclockwise on the ball of your base leg foot. Bring your kicking leg up and across your body at approximately a 45-degree angle to your left (your opponents right), while keeping your kicking leg and knee (10) straight, but not locked. This will place 100% of your weight onto your base leg. Remember to keep your base leg knee (9) slightly bent. As soon as your kicking foot

*Begin Arc
Foot Position*

leaves the ground, it should already be in the correct position to strike your opponent. As your kicking leg begins its upward "Path of Trajectory," your upper body (12a) should start turning in a counterclockwise direction so that the front of your body (12a) will be facing at approximately a 45-degree angle to the right of your opponent. In this position, the kicking leg side of your body should be closer to your opponent than your base leg side.

Your hands (13a) and elbows (13b) should still be in relatively the same position as they were in fighting position. That is like a boxer's with the lead hand held up at head level and away from your face about 8 to 12 inches (toward your opponent). Your lead elbow should be tucked in along your side in order to protect your ribs and stomach area. Your rear hand is held up alongside your cheek or neck, with the palm of that hand facing toward your cheek. Your rear elbow is also tucked in along your side in order to protect your ribs and stomach area.

Your back (12b) should be straight, but not rigid, and facing away from your opponent. You should not be hunched over or bent forward at the waist.

Your head (14) is facing straight ahead, and focused on your opponent's chest like a flashlight, not a laser beam. Your chin is tucked down behind your base leg shoulder, and your eyes (15) should still be centered on your opponent's chest.

Note: When you execute the "Begin Arc" phase of a Back Leg Crescent Kick, you will bring your kicking leg up and across your body to your left at approximately a 45-degree angle to the 7 o'clock position (1). However, your base leg will remain in relatively the same position. Remember, your view of the clock will be standing in front of it and looking at it. Therefore, when kicking with the right leg, your kicking leg and foot will move in a clockwise direction, and counterclockwise when kicking with the left leg.

Front View

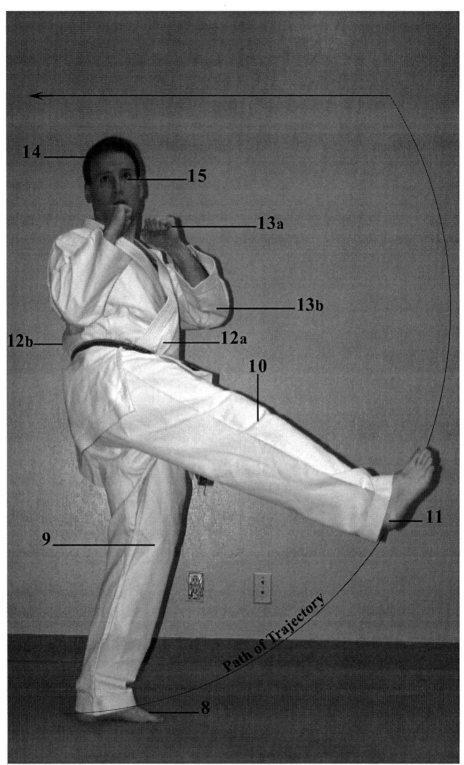

14

15

13a

13b

12b

12a

10

9

11

Path of Trajectory

8

Begin Arc Front View

Begin Arc Side View

41

Peak of Arc:

As your kicking leg and foot continue along their upward "Path of Trajectory," your base foot (16) which now bears 100% of your weight after shifting the weight onto it in order to initiate the kick, should now pivot approximately 45-degrees counterclockwise by pivoting on the ball of the foot.

The base leg knee (17) remains slightly bent in the direction of the toes of the base foot. Your kicking leg and foot (19) has now moved up to your opponent's head height by continuing along the upward "Path of Trajectory," while maintaining ap-

*Peak of Arc
Foot Position*

proximately a 45-degree angle to your left (your opponents right). Your toes should be pointed straight up in the air and flexed back towards your kicking leg knee,. So that with your leg extended, the outside edge of your heel will strike the target rather than the ankle or your toes. Your kicking leg and knee (18) should remain straight, but not locked. Once your kicking foot (19) has left the ground, it should remain in the correct striking position throughout the entire kick until returning back to the ground. After your foot has left the ground, the muscles in your thigh contract to bring your leg up into the "Peak of Arc" position.

Your upper body (20a) should remain facing at approximately a 45-degree angle to the right of your opponent. Your back (20b) should remain straight, but not rigid, while leaning back slightly.

Too many martial artists are sacrificing a proper upward "Path of Trajectory" in order to get the kick to the "Peak of Arc" and therefore, to the target faster. Although it is true to a certain extent that a kick will get to the "Peak of Arc" and therefore, to the target faster without utilizing the correct upward "Path of Trajectory," it is incorrect and can prove potentially harmful to the individual kicker. Proper technique should never be sacrificed for the sake of speed.

Your hands (21a) and elbows (21b), are also in relatively the same position as in (13a) and (13b), although they will occasionally change position to coincide with the various changes in body position, which take place throughout the execution of this kick. Your head (22) remains in the same position as in (14). Your eyes (23) are still focused on your opponent's chest like a flashlight, not a laser beam.

**Note: With your base leg remaining in rela-
tively the same position, your kicking
leg leaves the "Begin Arc" position (1),
and continues its (clockwise) upward
"Path of Trajectory" as it increases in
elevation to the correct target height.
This is called the "Peak of Arc" (2) and
is located midway between the 10 and
11 o'clock position. Depending upon
the height of your intended target.**

Front View

42

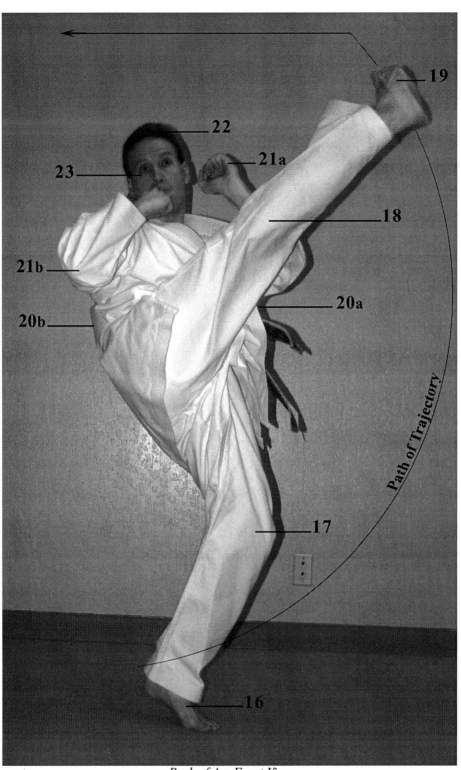

Peak of Arc Front View

Peak of Arc Side View

Impact:

Changing direction, you will pivot clockwise on the ball of your base leg foot (24) approximately 30-degrees from the previous position, so that your big toe is now closer to your opponent than your heel. After your foot has reached this position, it should now be pushing against the floor, while simultaneously gripping the floor with the entire foot. In other words, your entire foot should be in solid contact with the ground while the inside edge of your foot faces at approximately a 30-degree angle towards your opponent. Your base leg knee (25) is now straightened at the moment of impact to add power to the kick.

Impact
Foot Position

The outside edge of your kicking foot heel (27) should now be making contact with the appropriate, vital or vulnerable point, in one of the selected target areas on your opponent. Remember, that the contact time between your striking implement and the opponent's target area is minimal. Do not hit the target area and bounce off, or slow down. Strike through the target in an explosive, penetrating manner. Like a bullet!

At the moment of impact, your kicking leg knee (26) should be slightly (but not noticeably) bent in order to absorb the initial shock of impact. The entire kicking leg, as well as, your shoulders, back, hips, base leg, and head, should all be in a straight line. Upon initial impact, your entire body will tighten up to add power to the kick, and then immediately relax again, in order to facilitate a faster more explosive "Follow Through." Your kicking foot (27) and kicking knee (26), remain perpendicular to the ground with your toes pointed up, and continuing to travel along the straight and level "Path of Trajectory" from the "Peak of Arc" to "Impact" and continuing through to the "Follow Through" position.

I cannot stress enough the importance of utilizing the proper relaxation and tension principles outlined in this book when executing this or any other kick, strike or punch.

The front of your upper body (28a), which is now moving in a clockwise direction, is now facing directly at your opponent. Your upper body (28a) and back (28b) should remain straight but not rigid, while leaning back slightly. The kicking leg side of your body is still slightly closer to your opponent than your base leg side.

Your hands (29a) and elbows (29b), should still be up in relatively the same position as before in (21a) and (21b). Do not let them fly all over like a bird flapping its wings. Keep the elbows in to protect the rib cage and your hands up to protect your head. Your head (30) is still up with the chin tucked in behind the kicking leg shoulder. Your eyes (31) should still be looking over your kicking leg shoulder and focused on your opponent's chest.

Proper technique should never be sacrificed for the sake of speed. Remember the fable about the tortoise and the hare!

Front View

Front View

Note: As you look at the illustrations presented above, imagine that your are continuing to move in a clockwise motion from the "Peak of Arc" (2). Your kicking leg and foot will travel on a straight and level "Path of Trajectory" to the initial "Impact" (3) and subsequent "Strike Through" (4) of your target. The impact side of your target is represented by the outside edge of the number 1 (at the 12 o'clock position), while the "Strike Through" side of your target is represented by the outside edge of the number 2 (at the 12 o'clock position).

Remember, that although the illustrations of the clock show your kicking foot traveling in a circular motion throughout the entire kick, this is not correct. You kicking foot will only travel in a circular motion from the initial "Fighting Position" to the "Peak of Arc" and from the "Follow Through" position back down to your original starting position. From the "Peak of Arc" through "Impact" to the "Follow Through" position, your kicking foot should travel along a straight and level path.

Note: Look closely at the front and side view photographs of the "Impact" position, do you see anything out-of-place or incorrect? Look again! Notice how the heel on my base leg foot is not in contact with the ground during the "Impact" phase of the kick. This is perhaps one of the most common error committed by a person when executing a kick. Kicking while balancing on the ball of the foot rather than having the entire foot in contact with the ground is not only incorrect, but it also greatly reduces the effectiveness of the kick itself. I have purposely demonstrated this throughout this entire book to point out this most common error, and to emphasize the importance of <u>the proper foot positioning of your base leg foot throughout the entire kicking process.</u>

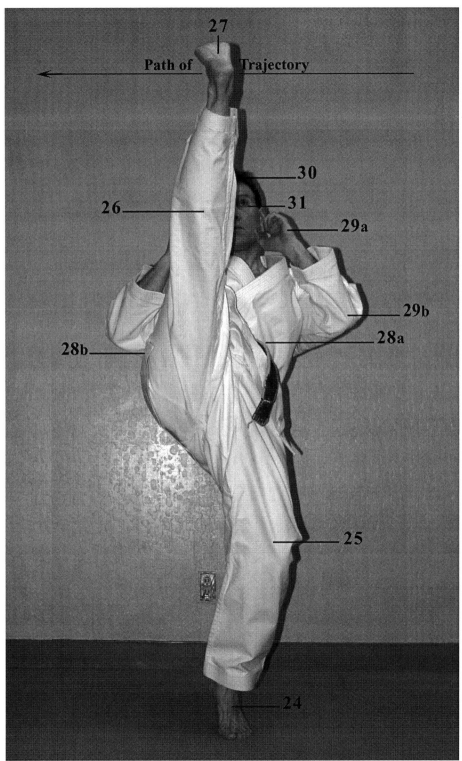

27

Path of ← Trajectory

30

31

26

29a

29b

28a

28b

25

24

Impact Front View

27———

30———

31——

29a———

26———————

29b

28b

28a

25

24

Impact Side View

48

Follow Through:

Depending on your foot position during "Impact," your base leg foot (32) will either continue to pivot approximately 30-degrees clockwise, or it will remain in contact with the ground and gripping it, while in approximately the same position it was in during "Impact." In either case, the base leg knee (33) returns to the slightly bent position, with it bending once again in the direction of the toes of the base foot. The kicking leg knee (34) remains slightly bent, and as with your kicking leg foot (35), should be approximately 45-degrees past your opponent,

Follow Through
Foot Position

as well as remaining perpendicular to the ground as it finishes traveling along the straight and level "Path of Trajectory." The toes on your kicking foot (35) should still be pointed up in the air and flexed back towards your kicking leg knee, exposing the outside edge of your heel as the striking implement. This can clearly be seen in both the front and side view photographs of the "Follow Through" position.

Too many martial artists seem to have a tendency to leave their kicks "hanging" in the air after executing a kick, rather than completing their kicks and returning them back down to the ground. My instructors used to call this "posing your kicks." This is an **extremely bad habit** to get into and one that needs to be corrected immediately. Another tendency that a lot of martial artists have, is to sacrifice a proper "Follow Through" in order to get the kick back on the ground faster. Although it is true to a certain extent that a kick will get to the ground faster without a proper "Follow Through" after "Impact," it can lead to potential problems.

Your upper body (36a) should still be facing directly towards your opponent, with the kicking leg side of your body slightly closer to your opponent than your base leg side. Your back (36b) remains straight but not rigid, and is facing away from your opponent, while continuing to lean back slightly.

Your hands (37a) and elbows (37b), are also in relatively the same position as they were in (29a) and (29b). Although, if you look at my left arm in the "Front View" photograph, you can see that it is a little too far away from my body.

Your head (38) remains in relatively the same position that it has been in throughout the entire kick. Your eyes (39), if you executed the kick properly, should be still be on your opponent, although they may not be focused on your opponent's chest if you have knocked him down. **Never take your eyes off of your opponent.**

Note: With your base leg remaining in relatively the same position, your kicking leg, after it leaves the initial "Impact" (3) and "Strike Through" (4) of your target, continues along its (clockwise) straight and level "Path of Trajectory" to the "Follow Through" position (5). Which is located at approximately a 45-degree angle to your right, and midway between the 1 and 2 o'clock positions.

Front View

35

36b

38

39

37a

34

36a

37b

Path of Trajectory

33

32

Follow Through Front View

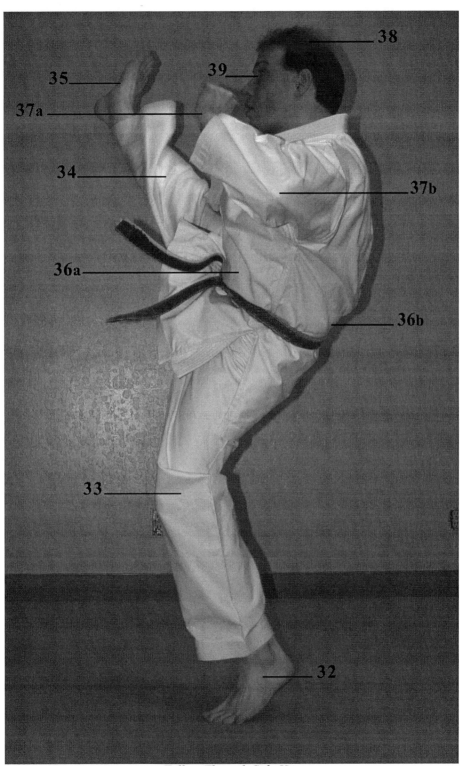

Follow Through Side View

End of Arc:

Once again, depending on your foot position during the "Impact" phase of the kick, your base leg foot (40) will continue to pivot anywhere from 30 to 90-degrees clockwise. Regardless of how far your base leg continues to pivot, your base leg knee (41) remains slightly bent. Your base leg continues to bear 100% of your weight until the kicking leg returns to your original "Fighting Position."

*End of Arc
Foot Position*

The kicking leg foot (43), should be at approximately a 45-degree angle to your right (your opponent's left) and at the height of your base leg knee. While it continues along its circular clockwise "Path of Trajectory," while decreasing in elevation as it returns to its original starting position. Your kicking leg remains straight with the kicking leg knee (42) slightly bent.

Often times, a martial artist will tend to slow down his/her kick after striking their target. This results in your kicking foot staying in the air much longer than necessary while continuing to balance on your base leg. This makes it much harder for you to follow up with another kick or technique, and it leaves you much more vulnerable to attack from your opponent.

Always remember, that your kicking foot should travel from the target back to its original starting position just as fast, if not faster, than it did from its initial fighting position to the target.

Your upper body (44a) should now be squared and facing directly towards your opponent. Your back (44b) remains straight but not rigid, and is facing directly away from your opponent, although you should no longer be leaning back slightly.

Your hands (45a) and elbows (45b), are also in relatively the same position as they were in (37a) and (37b).

Your head (46) remains in relatively the same position that it has been in throughout the entire kick. Your eyes (47), if you executed the kick properly, should be still be on your opponent, although they may not be focused on your opponent's chest if you have knocked him down. **Never take your eyes off of your opponent.**

Note: After reaching the "Follow Through" position (5), your kicking leg will decrease in elevation while continuing its circular clockwise motion. This is called the "End of Arc" (6), and is located at approximately the height of your base leg knee. Your kicking leg will then complete its circular path by returning to its original "Fighting Position."

Front View

46

47

45a

45b

44b

44a

42

43

Path of Trajectory

41

40

End of Arc Front View

53

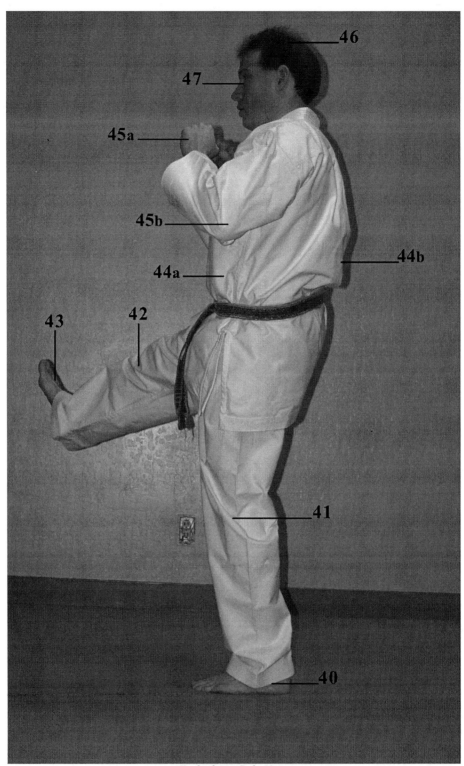

End of Arc Side View

Return to Fighting Position #1:

After you have reached the "End of Arc" position, simply return your kicking foot back to its original starting position. Your head, shoulders and hips will all come back around to your original "Fighting Position" before your kicking leg foot touches the ground. Your entire body should be upright and straight although not rigid throughout the entire return to your original "Fighting Position."

Once you return to a "Fighting Position," your fighting stance should once again be approximately shoulder width apart with the toes of your front or lead foot (48a) pointed directly at your opponent. The heel of your lead foot (48a) should be in a direct

Position #1

line with the heel of your rear foot (48b). The toes of your back or rear foot (48b) should be pointed away from your body at a 45-degree angle. For example, if your right foot were in the rear position, then the toes of that foot would be pointed to the right at a 45-degree angle. If the left foot were in the rear position, then the toes of your left foot would be pointed to the left at a 45-degree angle.

Your weight should once again be distributed over the balls of both feet and not over the entire surface area of the feet. The weight distribution over your feet should be approximately 55% over the lead leg and 45% over the rear leg.

Your knees (49) should be slightly but not noticeably bent. The lead leg knee should be slightly bent over the lead leg foot in the direction of the toes. The same also holds true for the rear knee in the fact that it too should be slightly bent over the rear foot in the direction of the rear toes. The bending of the knees contributes to faster movement with the legs as they are not locked straight or rigid and have better mobility when slightly bent rather than straight.

Your body (50) is facing at a 45-degree angle to your opponent. Your hands (51a) and elbows (51b), should still be held up like a boxer's, that is with the lead hand held up at head level and away from your face about 8 to 12 inches (toward your opponent). Your lead elbow should be tucked in along your side in order to protect your ribs and stomach area. Your rear hand is held up alongside your cheek with the palm of that hand facing toward your cheek. Your rear elbow is also tucked in along your side in order to protect your ribs and stomach area.

Your back (52) should be straight but not rigid and your lead shoulder should be raised up slightly in order to protect your chin.

Your head (53) is facing toward your opponent with the chin tucked down behind your upraised lead shoulder. Your eyes (54) should focus like a flashlight on the chest or center of your opponent whether he is still standing or not. At the same time, allow your peripheral vision to scan the rest of your opponent's body and therefore any movements he will make. I cannot stress this enough, **do not** become fixated on a particular spot or point of focus on your opponent. This becomes more of a hindrance than an asset when fighting.

55

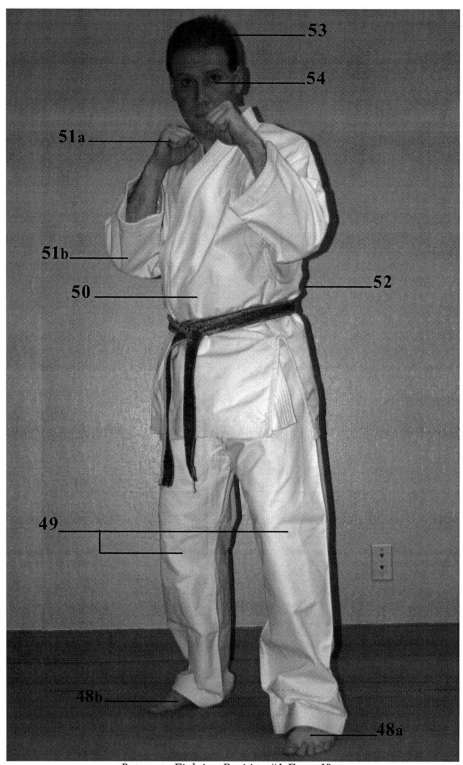

Return to Fighting Position #1 Front View

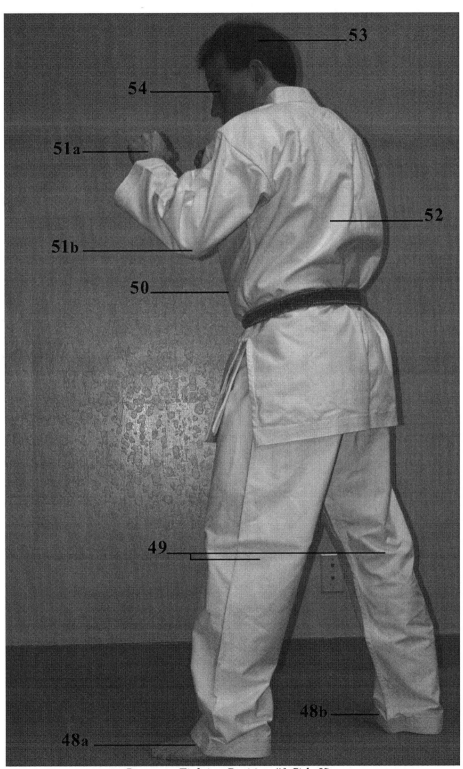

Return to Fighting Position #1 Side View

Return to Fighting Position #2:

After you have reached the "End of Arc" position, simply set your kicking foot down in front of you and toward your opponent, while simultaneously pivoting approximately 45-degrees counterclockwise on the ball of your base leg foot. Your kicking leg will now be in the forward position rather than in the rearward position. Your head, shoulders and hips will all move into another fighting position before your kicking leg foot touches the ground in front of you.

Position #2

Your entire body should be upright and straight although not rigid throughout the entire return to your new "Fighting Position." Remember that by stepping forward after this kick, you may be putting yourself in a more dangerous position because you are stepping in toward your opponent, putting you closer to him. **Be extra cautious when executing this move!**

Once you return to a "Fighting Position," your fighting stance should once again be approximately shoulder width apart with the toes of your front or lead foot (55a) pointed directly at your opponent. The heel of your lead foot (55a) should be in a direct line with the heel of your rear foot (55b). The toes of your back or rear foot (55b) should be pointed away from your body at a 45-degree angle. For example, if your left foot were in the rear position, then the toes of that foot would be pointed to the left at a 45-degree angle. If the right foot were in the rear position, then the toes of your right foot would be pointed to the right at a 45-degree angle. Your weight should be distributed over the balls of both feet and not over the entire surface area of the feet.

Your knees (56) should be slightly but not noticeably bent. The lead leg knee should be slightly bent over the lead leg foot in the direction of the toes. The same also holds true for the rear knee in the fact that it too should be slightly bent over the rear foot in the direction of the rear toes. The bending of the knees contributes to faster movement with the legs as they are not locked straight or rigid and have better mobility when slightly bent rather than straight.

Your body (57) is facing at a 45-degree angle to your opponent. Your hands (58a) and elbows (58b), should still be held up like a boxer's, that is with the lead hand held up at head level and away from your face about 8 to 12 inches (toward your opponent). Your lead elbow should be tucked in along your side in order to protect your ribs and stomach area. Your rear hand is held up alongside your cheek with the palm of that hand facing toward your cheek. Your rear elbow is also tucked in along your side in order to protect your ribs and stomach area.

Your back (59) should be straight but not rigid and your lead shoulder should be raised up slightly in order to protect your chin.

Your head (60) is facing toward your opponent with the chin tucked down behind your upraised lead shoulder. Your eyes (61) should focus like a flashlight on the chest or center of your opponent whether he is still standing or not. At the same time, allow your peripheral vision to scan the rest of your opponent's body.

Return to Fighting Position #2 Front View

Return to Fighting Position #2 Side View

Pictorial Overview:

Fighting Position	*Begin Arc*	*Peak of Arc*
Impact	*Follow Through*	*End of Arc*

Position #1	*Position #2*

Note: The following illustration, is a visual overview of the "Reverse Crescent Kick" clock, showing the sequence of events for the correct execution of a Back Leg Reverse Crescent Kick executed with the right leg. The center of the clock (pivot point for the minute hand) represents your hips. The hour hand represents your base leg, while the minute hand represents your kicking leg.

(1) Begin Arc Position, (2) Peak of Arc, (3) Initial Impact, (4) Strike Through, (5) Follow Through, (6) End of Arc, and finally, back to Fighting Position.

Variations of the Back Leg Reverse Crescent Kick

This chapter will explain in detail how to properly execute ten variations of the Back Leg Reverse Crescent Kick. Remember that all of these variations are derived from the primary kick, Back Leg Reverse Crescent Kick. Therefore, it is essential that you learn Back Leg Reverse Crescent Kick first before attempting any of these other variations.

To perhaps give you a better understanding of what I mean, let me use the comparison of building a house. Before you start building your house you are first going to need a set of blueprints, this would be the equivalent of the material presented in this book. Next you are going to need the proper materials to begin building with, this would be the equivalent of properly warming-up and stretching before you attempt to practice these kicks.

Next comes the hardest part for students to understand, now in order for your house to be stable, sturdy and secure you must first have a very well built and strong foundation. The foundation of your house is made out of concrete, while the foundation of this particular type of kick is, the Back Leg Reverse Crescent Kick. Once you have a strong and proficient Back Leg Reverse Crescent Kick, then you can begin to build upon that with the many different variations of that kick. Just like you would build your frame, walls, ceilings, floors and roof of your house.

If you don't take the time to first build a strong and stable foundation, your kicking skills along with your house, will not last and will collapse when the first strong storm or self-defense situation comes along.

As a general rule of thumb, every time you practice one of the variations of Back Leg Reverse Crescent Kick, you should practice Back Leg Reverse Crescent Kick itself at least ten times. I promise you that if you do this, all of your Reverse Crescent Kicks will steadily improve and become stronger.

Turning Reverse Crescent Kick

The Turning Reverse Crescent Kick is identical in execution to the Back Leg Reverse Crescent Kick, with one notable exception. A 360-degree circular turning motion, which is initiated immediately prior to executing the kick. This turning motion is used to either draw your opponent into you, or to confuse your opponent. It can also increase the power in this kick due to the added momentum of turning. The starting or fighting position for this kick is exactly the same at it was for Back Leg Reverse Crescent Kick, with your kicking leg in the rearward position rather than in the forward position. The actual turning motion prior to the execution of the kick, is performed by simply pivoting clockwise on the ball of your lead or base leg foot, while simultaneously sliding your kicking leg foot over approximately 8 inches in a clockwise direction. When executing the turning motion, be sure and move your base leg foot and kicking foot without initially moving your hips and upper body in order to avoid telegraphing the movement to your opponent. Your hips and upper body will begin to move as you start turning.

Fighting Position:

1. Your fighting position for this kick is exactly the same as it was for Back Leg Reverse Crescent Kick. With your kicking leg in the rearward position to begin with rather than in the forward position.
2. This stance is approximately shoulder width apart with the heel of your rear foot in a direct line with the heel of your front foot.
3. Your front or lead foot should be pointing directly at your opponent.
4. Your rear foot is angled towards the left at approximately a 45-degree angle. Your weight should be distributed evenly over the balls of both feet.
5. Your knees are slightly, but not noticeably bent. They should not be locked or rigid.
6. Your body should be facing at a 45-degree angle toward your opponent. This presents a smaller target area and also facilitates a faster turn, which allows you the opportunity to initiate a faster kick.
7. Your hands should be held up (like a boxer's), with the elbows tucked in to protect the ribs and your hands up to protect your head. Your hands should remain as close to this position as possible throughout the entire kick.
8. Your head should be facing your opponent with your chin tucked down and protected by your lead shoulder.

Fighting Position
Foot Position

Fighting Position Front View

Fighting Position Side View

64

9. Your eyes should be centered on your opponents chest.

Turn Back:

10. Turn 180-degrees clockwise by pivoting on the ball of your base leg foot so that your lead foot heel is now pointed directly at your opponent. While you are doing this, your rear foot is going to slide over approximately 8 inches while also turning 135-degrees clockwise so that the rear or kicking leg heel is also pointed directly at your opponent, while the toes of both feet are facing directly away from your opponent. Both knees are slightly, but not noticeably bent.

11. Your back should be straight and facing directly towards your opponent (at the 12 o'clock position), with the shoulder of your kicking leg slightly forward and toward your opponent.

12. Your hands and elbows should still be in relatively the same position as they were in the previous "Fighting Position."

13. Your head is turned so that you are looking over your kicking leg shoulder. Your chin is tucked down behind your kicking leg shoulder, and your eyes should still be centered on your opponent's chest.

Turn Back
Foot Position

Note: Your head should always turn first when executing any turning kick, so that you can maintain constant eye contact with your opponent.

Turning Position Front View

Turning Position Side View

Begin Arc:

14. Using the toes of your kicking foot, push off the floor and bring your kicking leg up at approximately a 45-degree angle. Your leg should be straight, and your kicking foot should already be in the correct position to strike your opponent.

15. As your bring your kicking leg up, your upper body should continue turning 360-degrees clockwise as it begins to face towards your opponent. Your back will remain straight, but not rigid.

16. Although your hands have switched position, they should still be held up (like a boxer's), with the elbows tucked in to protect the ribs and your hands up to protect your head.

17. Your head is up and facing towards your opponent, while your eyes continue to remain in contact with your opponent throughout the entire kick.

*Begin Arc
Foot Position*

Note: If you had an overhead view of the "Turning" portion of this technique, it would resemble a "smiley face." The number 1, in the illustration on the right, represents the position your kicking foot is in prior to the turn. The number 2 represents the position of your kicking foot after completing the turn.

Begin Arc Front View   *Begin Arc Side View*

Peak of Arc:

18. Your base leg foot should now have moved approximately 45-degrees clockwise by pivoting on the ball of your foot, while the knee on your base leg remains slightly bent. Your kicking leg has now moved up to your opponent's head height, although still at a 45-degree angle to your opponents right.

Peak of Arc
Foot Position

19. Your kicking foot remains in the correct striking position throughout the entire sequence.

20. Your upper body, with the kicking leg side of your body remaining closer to your opponent than your base leg side, continues to move in a clockwise direction and should be facing at approximately a 45-degree angle to the right of your opponent, while continuing to lean back slightly.

21. Your head should still be up and facing towards your opponent, while your eyes continue to remain in contact with your opponent throughout the entire kick.

Note: Your kicking foot will make a complete 360-degree circle throughout the entire execution of a Turning Reverse Crescent Kick, from your initial "Fighting Position" to "Return to Fighting Position." This is done while simultaneously increasing the elevation of the kicking foot to the correct target height by the time it reaches the "Peak of Arc" position, and decreasing the elevation from the "Follow Through" position, until the foot returns to its original starting position.

Peak of Arc Front View

Peak of Arc Side View

Impact:

22. Your base leg foot should now have moved approximately another 45-degrees (clockwise) by pivoting on the ball of your foot. At the moment of impact, your entire base leg foot should be in contact with the ground and gripping it.

Impact Foot Position

23. Your upper body, with the kicking leg side of your body remaining closer to your opponent than your base leg side, should now be facing almost directly at your opponent, while continuing to lean back slightly. At the moment of impact, your entire body should tighten to add power to the kick, as your foot continues to travel on a straight and level "Path of Trajectory" through the target.

24. Notice how your kicking foot, kicking leg, hips, back, shoulders, and head are all in alignment at the initial moment of "Impact." Also, notice how the toes of the kicking foot are pulled back towards your body and pointed up. This helps insure that contact with the target is made with the outside edge of your heel, not your ankle!

25. Your head should still be facing towards your opponent. Eye contact with your opponent is maintained at all times.

Note: Your kicking leg should be just as fast, if not faster, traveling from "Impact" to "Return to Fighting Position," than it is traveling from "Fighting Position" to "Impact."

Impact Front View

Impact Side View

Follow Through:

26. Depending on your foot position during "Impact," your base leg foot will either continue to pivot approximately 30-degrees clockwise, or it will remain in contact with the ground and gripping it, while in approximately the same position it was in during "Impact." In either case, the knee on your base leg will remain slightly bent.

Follow Through
Foot Position

27. Your upper body is now facing directly towards your opponent and leaning back slightly. Although your body is in this position, your back will remain straight but not rigid.

28. Your kicking leg foot should continue along exactly the same straight and level path it followed from the "Peak of Arc" to "Impact." Your foot should still remain at your opponent's head height, although it should now be at a 45-degree angle to your opponents left.

29. Your head should still be facing towards your opponent. Eye contact with your opponent is maintained at all times.

Note: Your "Peak of Arc" should be at the exact same height as your intended target, and should travel along a straight and level path from the "Peak of Arc" through "Impact" to the "Follow Through" position.

Follow Through Front View

Follow Through Side View

End of Arc:

30. Once again, depending on your foot position during the "Impact" phase of the kick, your base leg foot will continue to pivot anywhere from 30 to 90-degrees clockwise. Regardless of how far your base leg continues to pivot, the knee on your base leg will remain slightly bent.

31. Your kicking leg remains straight with the knee slightly bent. Your kicking foot is now at approximately a 45-degree angle to your right (your opponent's left), at approximately the height of your base leg knee.

*End of Arc
Foot Position*

32. Your upper body, with the base leg side of your body now closer to your opponent than your kicking leg side, should now be facing at approximately a 45-degree angle to the left of your opponent, although you should no longer be leaning back. Your back should be straight, but not rigid.

33. Your head should still be up with your eyes looking directly at your opponent, whether he is still standing, or lying on the ground.

*Clockwise
with the Right Leg*

Note: If you look closely at the illustration on the right, you will see that from your initial "Fighting Position", you will pivot on the ball of your base leg foot approximately 270-degrees clockwise, before setting your entire foot back down...

End of Arc Front View   *End of Arc Side View*

Return to Fighting Position:

34. Your entire body from your head to your toes, continues the 360-degree clockwise motion and should now be in exactly the same fighting position that you were in prior to executing this kick.

35. Your kicking leg foot also continues the 360-degree clockwise motion and returns to its original starting position. Your kicking leg knee will remain slightly bent as it returns to the starting position.

36. Your hands, which should have remained as close to this position as possible throughout the entire kick, are held up (like a boxer's), with the elbows tucked in to protect the ribs and your hands up to protect your head.

37. Your head should now be looking over your lead leg shoulder with your eyes in contact with your opponent.

Return to Fighting Position Foot Position

Counterclockwise with the Left Leg

Note: ...on the ground at the initial moment of impact. Immediately after the initial moment of impact, you will complete the 360-degree turn and return to your original starting position by pivoting the remaining 90-degrees on the ball of your base leg foot. When kicking with the left foot, you will move counterclockwise.

Return to Fighting Position Front View   *Return to Fighting Position Side View*

Pictorial Overview:

Fighting Position   *Turn*   *Begin Arc*

Peak of Arc   *Impact*   *Follow Through*

End of Arc   *Return to Fighting Position*

Spinning Reverse Crescent Kick

The Spinning Reverse Crescent Kick is identical in execution to the Turning Reverse Crescent Kick, with one notable exception. A stepping forward motion, which is performed prior to executing the kick. This step is used to close the distance with ones opponent and can also increase the power in this kick due to the added momentum obtained from stepping forward. The actual spinning motion of the rearward foot prior to execution of the kick is performed by simply stepping forward with the rearward foot into another fighting position. This will now put your kicking leg in the rearward position. When executing the step forward/spinning motion, be sure and move your rearward foot without initially moving your hips and upper body in order to avoid telegraphing the movement to your opponent. Your hips and upper body will begin to move as you set your foot back down on the ground.

Fighting Position:

1. Your fighting position for this kick is exactly the same as it will be for Step-Back Turning Reverse Crescent Kick, with your kicking leg in the forward position to begin with rather than in the rearward position.
2. This stance is approximately shoulder width apart with the heel of your rear foot directly in line with the heel of your front foot.
3. Your front or lead foot should be pointed directly at your opponent.
4. Your rear foot is angled toward the left at approximately a 45-degree angle. Your weight should be distributed evenly over the balls of both feet.

Fighting Position Foot Position

Fighting Position Front View

Fighting Position Side View

5. Your knees are slightly, but not noticeably bent. They should not be locked straight or rigid.
6. Your body should be facing at a 45-degree angle towards your opponent. This presents a smaller target area and also facilitates a faster step-and-turn, which allows you the opportunity to initiate a faster kick.
7. Your hands should be held up (like a boxer's), with the elbows tucked in to protect the ribs and your hands up to protect your head. Your hands should remain as close to this position as possible throughout the entire kick.
8. Your head should be facing your opponent with your chin tucked down and protected by your lead shoulder.
9. Your eyes should be centered on your opponent's chest.

Step Forward & Turn Back:
10. Take a step forward with your rear foot. And...
11. As you step forward with your rear leg, pivot on the ball of your base leg foot. This will have the effect of turning your back toward your opponent.
12. Your eyes should still be centered on your opponent's chest
13. When you set your rear foot down, it should be not only in front of you, but also approximately 8 inches to the side. This allows for better balance and a more accurate kick. Your back should now be toward your opponent, and the heel of your now-base leg foot should also be pointed toward your opponent.

Step Forward &
Turn Back
Foot Position

Step Forward & Turn Front View

Step Forward & Turn Side View

74

Begin Arc:

14. Using the toes of your kicking foot, push off the floor and bring your kicking leg up at approximately a 45-degree angle. Your leg should be straight, and your kicking foot should already be in the correct position to strike your opponent.

15. As your bring your kicking leg up, your upper body should continue turning 360-degrees clockwise as it begins to face towards your opponent. Your back will remain straight, but not rigid.

16. Although your hands have switched position, they should still be held up (like a boxer's), with the elbows tucked in to protect the ribs and your hands up to protect your head.

17. Your head is up and facing towards your opponent, while your eyes continue to remain in contact with your opponent throughout the entire kick.

Begin Arc
Foot Position

Note: When executing a Turning or Spinning Reverse Crescent Kick, keep in mind that the primary key to the successful execution of this or any kick, especially a 360-degree circular kick, is the proper pivoting on the ball of the base leg foot throughout the entire execution of the kick.

Begin Arc Front View   *Begin Arc Side View*

Peak of Arc:

18. Your base leg foot should now have moved approximately 45-degrees clockwise by pivoting on the ball of your foot, while the knee on your base leg remains slightly bent. Your kicking leg has now moved up to your opponent's head height, although still at a 45-degree angle to your opponents right.

19. Your kicking foot remains in the correct striking position throughout the entire sequence.

20. Your upper body, with the kicking leg side of your body remaining closer to your opponent than your base leg side, continues to move in a clockwise direction and should be facing at approximately a 45-degree angle to the right of your opponent, while continuing to lean back slightly.

21. Your head should still be up and facing towards your opponent, while your eyes continue to remain in contact with your opponent throughout the entire kick.

Peak of Arc
Foot Position

Note: Although the Reverse Crescent Kick is used primarily to strike the head of an opponent at a high section level, you should also practice the Reverse Crescent Kick at a midsection (stomach) level, and low section (knee) level.

Peak of Arc Front View

Peak of Arc Side View

Impact:

22. Your base leg foot should now have moved approximately another 45-degrees (clockwise) by pivoting on the ball of your foot. At the moment of impact, your entire base leg foot should be in contact with the ground and gripping it.

Impact
Foot Position

23. Your upper body, with the kicking leg side of your body remaining closer to your opponent than your base leg side, should now be facing almost directly at your opponent, while continuing to lean back slightly. At the moment of impact, your entire body should tighten to add power to the kick, as your foot continues to travel on a straight and level "Path of Trajectory" through the target.

24. Notice how your kicking foot, kicking leg, hips, back, shoulders, and head are all in alignment at the initial moment of "Impact." Also, notice how the toes of the kicking foot are pulled back towards your body and pointed up. This helps insure that contact with the target is made with the outside edge of your heel, not your ankle!

25. Your head should still be facing towards your opponent. Eye contact with your opponent is maintained at all times.

Note: The head, which can easily be compared to the ever popular "bobblehead" dolls, makes for a difficult target with a kick due to the ease in which the head can "bob and weave" like a boxer in order to avoid being hit.

Impact Front View

Impact Side View

Follow Through:

26. Depending on your foot position during "Impact," your base leg foot will either continue to pivot approximately 30-degrees clockwise, or it will remain in contact with the ground and gripping it, while in approximately the same position it was in during "Impact." In either case, the knee on your base leg will remain slightly bent.

Follow Through Foot Position

27. Your upper body is now facing directly towards your opponent and leaning back slightly. Although your body is in this position, your back will remain straight but not rigid.

28. Your kicking leg foot should continue along exactly the same straight and level path it followed from the "Peak of Arc" to "Impact." Your foot should still remain at your opponent's head height, although it should now be at a 45-degree angle to your opponents left.

29. Your head should still be facing towards your opponent. Eye contact with your opponent is maintained at all times.

Note: If you leave your kicking foot hanging in the air after "STRIKING THROUGH" your target, you have not only executed the kick improperly, but you have also left yourself in a very vulnerable position. One that your opponent may very easily exploit to his advantage. As I have stated before, in order to maximize the effectiveness of your kicks, you must, correctly, apply <u>all of the proper principles outlined in this book</u>.

Follow Through Front View   *Follow Through Side View*

End of Arc:

30. Once again, depending on your foot position during the "Impact" phase of the kick, your base leg foot will continue to pivot anywhere from 30 to 90-degrees clockwise. Regardless of how far your base leg continues to pivot, the knee on your base leg will remain slightly bent.

End of Arc
Foot Position

31. Your kicking leg remains straight with the knee slightly bent. Your kicking foot is now at approximately a 45-degree angle to your right (your opponent's left), at approximately the height of your base leg knee.

32. Your upper body, with the base leg side of your body now closer to your opponent than your kicking leg side, should now be facing at approximately a 45-degree angle to the left of your opponent, although you should no longer be leaning back. Your back should be straight, but not rigid.

33. Your head should still be up with your eyes looking directly at your opponent, whether he is still standing, or lying on the ground.

Note: The only time your entire base leg foot is in contact with the ground, is in the initial "Fighting Position," during the "Impact" phase of the kick, and in the "Return to Fighting Position."

End of Arc Front View   *End of Arc Side View*

Return to Fighting Position:

34. Your entire body from your head to your toes, continues the 360-degree clockwise motion and should now be in exactly the same fighting position that you were in prior to executing this kick.

35. Your kicking leg foot also continues the 360-degree clockwise motion and returns to its original starting position. Your kicking leg knee will remain slightly bent as it returns to the starting position.

36. Your hands, which should have remained as close to this position as possible throughout the entire kick, are held up (like a boxer's), with the elbows tucked in to protect the ribs and your hands up to protect your head.

37. Your head should now be looking over your lead leg shoulder with your eyes in contact with your opponent.

Return to Fighting Position Foot Position

Note: Not pivoting correctly on the ball of your base leg foot, throughout the entire execution of any 360-degree circular kick, can be likened to the act of "ringing out" a wet hand towel. Each end of the towel is grasped firmly in each hand, then both hands twist the towel in opposite directions, which results in the tightening of the towel in the middle, creating a tremendous amount of pressure on the towel which forces the water out. This is exactly what happens to your knee when you fail to pivot properly on the ball of your base leg foot. However, unlike the towel who's pressure is slow and gradual, the pressure on your knee is sudden and EXPLOSIVE!

Return to Fighting Position Front View   *Return to Fighting Position Side View*

Pictorial Overview:

Fighting Position   Step Forward &...   Turn

Begin Arc   Peak of Arc   Impact

FollowThrough   End of Arc   Return to Fighting Position

Step-Back Turning Reverse Crescent Kick

The Step-Back Turning Reverse Crescent Kick is identical in execution to the Turning Reverse Crescent Kick, with one notable exception. A stepping backward motion, which is performed immediately prior to executing the kick. This stepping backward motion is used to either draw your opponent into you, or to avoid an attack. It can also increase the power in this kick due to the added momentum of stepping backward. The starting or fighting position for this kick begins with your kicking leg in the forward position rather than in the rear position. The actual stepping back motion of the forward foot prior to the execution of the kick, is performed by simply stepping back with the forward foot into another fighting position. Only now the kicking leg is in the rearward rather than the forward position. When executing the stepping back motion, be sure and move your forward foot without initially moving your hips and upper body in order to avoid telegraphing the movement to your opponent. Your hips and upper body will begin to move as you set your foot back down on the ground.

Fighting Position:

1. Your fighting position for this kick is exactly the same as it was for Spinning Reverse Crescent Kick, with your kicking leg in the forward position to begin with rather than in the rearward position.
2. This stance is approximately shoulder width apart with the heel of your rear foot in a direct line with the heel of your front foot.
3. Your front or lead foot should be pointing directly at your opponent.
4. Your rear foot is angled toward the left at approximately a

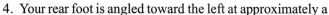

Fighting Position Foot Position

Fighting Position Front View

Fighting Position Side View

45-degree angle. Your weight is distributed evenly over the balls of both feet.

5. Your knees are slightly, but not noticeably bent. They should not be locked straight or rigid.

6. Your body should be facing at a 45-degree angle toward your opponent. This presents a smaller target area and also facilitates a faster step-back and turn, which allows you the opportunity to initiate a faster kick.

7. Your hands should be held up (like a boxers), with the elbows tucked in to protect the ribs and your hands up to protect your head. Your hands should remain as close to this position as possible throughout the entire kick.

8. Your head should be facing your opponent with your chin tucked down and protected by your lead shoulder.

9. Your eyes should be centered on your opponent's chest.

Step-Back & Turn Back:

10. Take a step backward with your front foot. And...

11. ...as you step backward with your front foot, pivot on the ball of your base leg. This will have the effect of turning your back towards your opponent.

12. While you are stepping back, and as you begin to turn, you should be turning your head and looking over your kicking leg shoulder at your opponent. Your eyes should be centered on your opponent's chest.

13. When you set your front foot down, only the ball of your kicking leg foot should be touching the

Step Back & Turn Back
Foot Position

Step Back & Turn Front View

Step Back & Turn Side View

83

ground. However, when initially learning this kick, make sure you have your entire kicking foot in contact with the ground. Your kicking foot should not only be behind you, but should also be approximately 8 inches to the side. This allows for better balance and a more accurate kick. Your back should now be toward your opponent, and the heel of your now-base leg foot should also be pointed toward your opponent.

Begin Arc:

14. Using the toes of your kicking foot, push off the floor and bring your kicking leg up at approximately a 45-degree angle. Your leg should be straight, and your kicking foot should already be in the correct position to strike your opponent.

15. As your bring your kicking leg up, your upper body should continue turning 360-degrees clockwise as it begins to face towards your opponent. Your back will remain straight, but not rigid.

16. Although your hands have switched position, they should still be held up (like a boxer's), with the elbows tucked in to protect the ribs and your hands up to protect your head.

17. Your head is up and facing towards your opponent, while your eyes continue to remain in contact with your opponent throughout the entire kick.

Begin Trajectory
Foot Position

Begin Arc Front View

Begin Arc Side View

Peak of Arc:

18. Your base leg foot should now have moved approximately 45-degrees clockwise by pivoting on the ball of your foot, while the knee on your base leg remains slightly bent. Your kicking leg has now moved up to your opponent's head height, although still at a 45-degree angle to your opponents right.

*Peak of Arc
Foot Position*

19. Your kicking foot remains in the correct striking position throughout the entire sequence.
20. Your upper body, with the kicking leg side of your body remaining closer to your opponent than your base leg side, continues to move in a clockwise direction and should be facing at approximately a 45-degree angle to the right of your opponent, while continuing to lean back slightly.
21. Your head should still be up and facing towards your opponent, while your eyes continue to remain in contact with your opponent throughout the entire kick.

Note: Not turning your upper body and lower body together in the same direction when executing any 360-degree kick, can also be likened to the act of "ringing out" a wet hand towel as previously described on page 80. However, the pressure is not on your knee in this case, but your lower back. Always adhere to proper form and technique when executing any kick, not just the 360-degree circular ones.

Peak of Arc Front View

Peak of Arc Side View

Impact:

22. Your base leg foot should now have moved approximately another 45-degrees (clockwise) by pivoting on the ball of your foot. At the moment of impact, your entire base leg foot should be in contact with the ground and gripping it.

Impact
Foot Position

23. Your upper body, with the kicking leg side of your body remaining closer to your opponent than your base leg side, should now be facing almost directly at your opponent, while continuing to lean back slightly. At the moment of impact, your entire body should tighten to add power to the kick, as your foot continues to travel on a straight and level "Path of Trajectory" through the target.

24. Notice how your kicking foot, kicking leg, hips, back, shoulders, and head are all in alignment at the initial moment of "Impact." Also, notice how the toes of the kicking foot are pulled back towards your body and pointed up. This helps insure that contact with the target is made with the outside edge of your heel, not your ankle!

25. Your head should still be facing towards your opponent. Eye contact with your opponent is maintained at all times.

Note: Don't over-extend your technique by "reaching" for your opponent. Create the proper distance using footwork before executing your kick.

Impact Front View   *Impact Side View*

Follow Through:

26. Depending on your foot position during "Impact," your base leg foot will either continue to pivot approximately 30-degrees clockwise, or it will remain in contact with the ground and gripping it, while in approximately the same position it was in during "Impact." In either case, the knee on your base leg will remain slightly bent.

27. Your upper body is now facing directly towards your opponent and leaning back slightly. Although your body is in this position, your back will remain straight but not rigid.

28. Your kicking leg foot should continue along exactly the same straight and level path it followed from the "Peak of Arc" to "Impact." Your foot should still remain at your opponent's head height, although it should now be at a 45-degree angle to your opponents left.

29. Your head should still be facing towards your opponent. Eye contact with your opponent is maintained at all times.

Follow Through
Foot Position

Note: If you are too slow in bringing your kicking leg from the "Peak of Arc" position through "Impact" to the "Follow Through" position, I guarantee you that your opponent will not be slow in grabbing it.

Follow Through Front View   *Follow Through Side View*

End of Arc:

30. Once again, depending on your foot position during the "Impact" phase of the kick, your base leg foot will continue to pivot anywhere from 30 to 90-degrees clockwise. Regardless of how far your base leg continues to pivot, the knee on your base leg will remain slightly bent.

31. Your kicking leg remains straight with the knee slightly bent. Your kicking foot is now at approximately a 45-degree angle to your right (your opponent's left), at approximately the height of your base leg knee.

32. Your upper body, with the base leg side of your body now closer to your opponent than your kicking leg side, should now be facing at approximately a 45-degree angle to the left of your opponent, although you should no longer be leaning back. Your back should be straight, but not rigid.

33. Your head should still be up with your eyes looking directly at your opponent, whether he is still standing, or lying on the ground.

*End of Arc
Foot Position*

Note: After you have become sufficiently proficient executing the kicks described in this book wearing gi pants and being barefoot, you will want to also start practicing them wearing your normal everyday clothes and shoes. There is a big difference between kicking in gi pants and barefoot, and kicking in everyday clothes and shoes.

End of Arc Front View *End of Arc Side View*

Return to Fighting Position:

34. Your entire body from your head to your toes, continues the 360-degree clockwise motion and should now be in exactly the same fighting position that you were in prior to executing this kick.

35. Your kicking leg foot also continues the 360-degree clockwise motion and returns to its original starting position. Your kicking leg knee will remain slightly bent as it returns to the starting position.

36. Your hands, which should have remained as close to this position as possible throughout the entire kick, are held up (like a boxer's), with the elbows tucked in to protect the ribs and your hands up to protect your head.

37. Your head should now be looking over your lead leg shoulder with your eyes in contact with your opponent.

Return to Fighting Position Foot Position

Note: The available vital and/or vulnerable points that are going to be open to attack on your opponent, is going to be determined by your opponent. However, you can create your own openings on your opponent not only by setting him up with various attack strategies (like a boxer utilizing the jab to set up a right cross or hook), but also by correctly utilizing deception prior to, and during your attack.

Return to Fighting Position Front View

Return to Fighting Position Side View

89

Pictorial Overview:

Fighting Position

Step Forward &...

Turn

Begin Arc

Peak of Arc

Impact

FollowThrough

End of Arc

Return to Fighting Position

Switch Turning Reverse Crescent Kick

The Switch Turning Reverse Crescent Kick is identical in execution to the Turning Reverse Crescent Kick, with one notable exception. A switching motion of the feet, which is performed immediately prior to the execution of the kick. The switch is used to confuse the opponent and can also increase the power in this kick due to the added momentum of switching your feet. The starting position is the same as for Spinning Reverse Crescent Kick, with your kicking leg in the forward position rather than in the rearward position. The actual switching of the feet prior to execution of the kick is performed by simultaneously switching the position of both feet utilizing a straight line or scissors type motion. With the end result being a fighting position with the kicking leg now in the rearward position. When executing the switch, be sure and move your feet first without initially moving your upper body in order to avoid telegraphing the switch to your opponent. Your hips and upper body will begin to move immediately after your feet, but not before.

Fighting Position:

1. Your fighting position for this kick is the exact same as it was for Spinning Reverse Crescent Kick. That is your kicking leg will be in the forward position to begin with rather than in the rearward position.
2. This stance is approximately shoulder width apart with the heel of your rear foot in a direct line with the heel of your front foot.
3. Your front or lead foot should be pointing directly at your opponent.
4. Your rear foot is angled towards the left at approximately a

Fighting Position Foot Position

Fighting Position Front View

Fighting Position Side View

45-degree angle. Your weight should be distributed evenlyover the balls of both feet.

5. Your knees are slightly, but not noticeably bent. They should not be locked or rigid.

6. Your body should be facing at a 45-degree angle toward your opponent. This presents a smaller target area and also facilitates a faster switch-and-turn, which allows you the opportunity to initiate a faster kick.

7. Your hands should be held up (like a boxer's), with the elbows tucked in to protect the ribs and your hands up to protect your head. Your hands should remain as close to this position as possible throughout the entire kick.

8. Your head should be facing your opponent with your chin tucked down and protected by your lead shoulder.

9. Your eyes should be centered on your opponents chest.

Switch Feet & Turn Back:

10. Utilizing a scissors type motion of your legs and feet, simultaneously switch your front foot with your rear foot. After you have begun the switching of the feet, turn your back towards your opponent. After switching, the heels of both of your feet should be pointed towards your opponent.

11. Prior to turning your back, your head should be turned over your kicking leg shoulder and your eyes should be looking at your opponent.

12. Your back should be facing directly toward your opponent.

Switch Feet & Turn Back Foot Position

Switch Feet & Turn Front View

Switch Feet & Turn Side View

Begin Arc:

13. Using the toes of your kicking foot, push off the floor and bring your kicking leg up at approximately a 45-degree angle. Your leg should be straight, and your kicking foot should already be in the correct position to strike your opponent.

14. As your bring your kicking leg up, your upper body should continue turning 360-degrees clockwise as it begins to face towards your opponent. Your back will remain straight, but not rigid.

15. Although your hands have switched position, they should still be held up (like a boxer's), with the elbows tucked in to protect the ribs and your hands up to protect your head.

16. Your head is up and facing towards your opponent, while your eyes continue to remain in contact with your opponent throughout the entire kick.

Begin Arc
Foot Position

Note: One of the most important factors needed for the correct execution of a Reverse Crescent Kick, or any kick for that matter, is the proper pivoting on the ball of the base leg foot throughout the entire execution of the kick.

Begin Arc Front View   *Begin Arc Side View*

Peak of Arc:

17. Your base leg foot should now have moved approximately 45-degrees clockwise by pivoting on the ball of your foot, while the knee on your base leg remains slightly bent. Your kicking leg has now moved up to your opponent's head height, although still at a 45-degree angle to your opponents right.

Peak of Arc
Foot Position

18. Your kicking foot remains in the correct striking position throughout the entire sequence.

19. Your upper body, with the kicking leg side of your body remaining closer to your opponent than your base leg side, continues to move in a clockwise direction and should be facing at approximately a 45-degree angle to the right of your opponent, while continuing to lean back slightly.

20. Your head should still be up and facing towards your opponent, while your eyes continue to remain in contact with your opponent throughout the entire kick.

Note: When executing a "Switch" kick of any kind, compare it to the shooting action of a rifle. For example; the switching motion is the trigger on the rifle, while the ground is the firing pin, the ball of your kicking foot is the primer in the bullet casing, the combination of muscular speed, strength and proper technique is the gunpowder, and finally, the heel of your kicking foot is the bullet. As you squeeze the trigger (switch your feet), it releases the firing pin striking the primer in the casing...

Peak of Arc Front View

Peak of Arc Side View

Impact:

21. Your base leg foot should now have moved approximately another 45-degrees (clockwise) by pivoting on the ball of your foot. At the moment of impact, your entire base leg foot should be in contact with the ground and gripping it.

*Impact
Foot Position*

22. Your upper body, with the kicking leg side of your body remaining closer to your opponent than your base leg side, should now be facing almost directly at your opponent, while continuing to lean back slightly. At the moment of impact, your entire body should tighten to add power to the kick, as your foot continues to travel on a straight and level "Path of Trajectory" through the target.

23. Notice how your kicking foot, kicking leg, hips, back, shoulders, and head are all in alignment at the initial moment of "Impact." Also, notice how the toes of the kicking foot are pulled back towards your body and pointed up. This helps insure that contact with the target is made with the outside edge of your heel, not your ankle!

24. Your head should still be facing towards your opponent. Eye contact with your opponent is maintained at all times.

Note: ...(the ball of your kicking foot touching the ground), and ignites the gunpowder, which fires the bullet (execute your kick) along its path of trajectory, where it <u>STRIKES THROUGH</u> its target.

Impact Front View *Impact Side View*

Follow Through:

25. Depending on your foot position during "Impact," your base leg foot will either continue to pivot approximately 30-degrees clockwise, or it will remain in contact with the ground and gripping it, while in approximately the same position it was in during "Impact." In either case, the knee on your base leg will remain slightly bent.

Follow Through Foot Position

26. Your upper body is now facing directly towards your opponent and leaning back slightly. Although your body is in this position, your back will remain straight but not rigid.

27. Your kicking leg foot should continue along exactly the same straight and level path it followed from the "Peak of Arc" to "Impact." Your foot should still remain at your opponent's head height, although it should now be at a 45-degree angle to your opponents left.

28. Your head should still be facing towards your opponent. Eye contact with your opponent is maintained at all times.

Note: The key to success in any endeavor you wish to pursue is this, self-discipline. Ask yourself this question, "Are you willing to do whatever you have to do, in order to get what you want?"

Follow Through Front View   *Follow Through Side View*

End of Arc:

29. Once again, depending on your foot position during the "Impact" phase of the kick, your base leg foot will continue to pivot anywhere from 30 to 90-degrees clockwise. Regardless of how far your base leg continues to pivot, the knee on your base leg will remain slightly bent.

End of Arc
Foot Position

30. Your kicking leg remains straight with the knee slightly bent. Your kicking foot is now at approximately a 45-degree angle to your right (your opponent's left), at approximately the height of your base leg knee.

31. Your upper body, with the base leg side of your body now closer to your opponent than your kicking leg side, should now be facing at approximately a 45-degree angle to the left of your opponent, although you should no longer be leaning back. Your back should be straight, but not rigid.

32. Your head should still be up with your eyes looking directly at your opponent, whether he is still standing, or lying on the ground.

Note: As a general rule-of-thumb, your initial impact point is at the surface of the target area (Vital/Vulnerable Point) in which you intend to <u>STRIKE THROUGH</u>. Your impact continues <u>THROUGH</u> the body or head, and ends outside of the body on the opposite side. Remember, DO NOT PUSH your opponent, <u>STRIKE THROUGH</u> your opponent.

End of Arc Front View

End of Arc Side View

Return to Fighting Position:

33. Your entire body from your head to your toes, continues the 360-degree clockwise motion and should now be in exactly the same fighting position that you were in after switching your feet and just prior to executing this kick.

34. Your kicking leg foot also continues the 360-degree clockwise motion and returns to its original starting position. Your kicking leg knee will remain slightly bent as it returns to the starting position.

35. Your hands, which should have remained as close to this position as possible throughout the entire kick, are held up (like a boxer's), with the elbows tucked in to protect the ribs and your hands up to protect your head.

36. Your head should now be looking over your lead leg shoulder with your eyes in contact with your opponent.

Return to Fighting Position Foot Position

Note: If you execute a Reverse Crescent Kick properly, you will exert a minimal amount of muscular effort during the upward and downward "Path of Trajectory" going from the initial "Fighting Position" all the way up to the "Peak of Arc," and from the "Follow Through" position back down to your original "Fighting Position." You will exert the maximum amount of muscular effort on the straight and level "Path of Trajectory" from the "Peak of Arc" to "Impact" and continuing through to the "Follow Through" position.

Return to Fighting Position Front View   *Return to Fighting Position Side View*

98

Pictorial Overview:

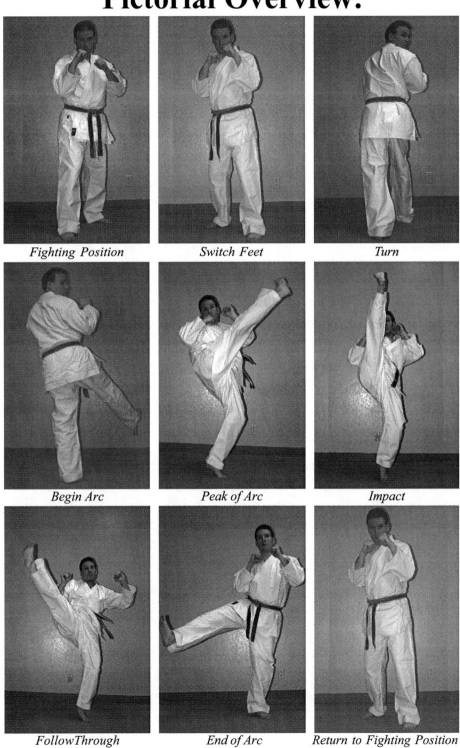

Fighting Position   Switch Feet   Turn

Begin Arc   Peak of Arc   Impact

FollowThrough   End of Arc   Return to Fighting Position

Hop/Slide Forward Reverse Crescent Kick

The Hopping/Sliding Forward Reverse Crescent Kick is identical in execution to the Back Leg Reverse Crescent Kick, with one notable exception. A hopping/sliding forward motion, which is performed immediately prior to executing the kick. This motion is used to close the distance between you and your opponent. It can also increase the power in this kick due to the added momentum of hopping/sliding forward. The actual hop or slide motion is performed by both feet simultaneously moving forward keeping the same distance between them. The hop or slide can be anywhere from a few inches up to 18 inches. Keep your hips and upper body as still as possible throughout the initial hop or slide forward in order to avoid telegraphing the move to your opponent.

Fighting Position:

1. Your fighting position for this kick is exactly the same as it was for Back Leg Reverse Crescent Kick. With your kicking leg in the rearward position to begin with rather than in the forward position.
2. This stance is approximately shoulder width apart with the heel of your rear foot in a direct line with the heel of your front foot.
3. Your front or lead foot should be pointing directly at your opponent.
4. Your rear foot is angled toward the right at approximately a 45-degree angle. Your weight should be distributed evenly over the balls of both feet.
5. Your knees are slightly, but not noticeably bent. They should not be locked straight or rigid.
6. Your body should be facing at a 45-degree angle toward

*Fighting Position
Foot Position*

Fighting Position Front View

Fighting Position Side View

your opponent. This presents a smaller target area and also facilitates a faster hop/slide forward, which allows you the opportunity to initiate a faster kick.

7. Your hands should be held up (like a boxers), with the elbows tucked in to protect the ribs and your hands up to protect your head. Your hands should remain as close to this position as possible throughout the entire kick.

8. Your head should be facing your opponent with your chin tucked down and protected by your lead shoulder.

9. Your eyes should be centered on your opponent's chest.

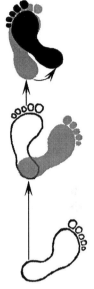

Hop/Slide Forward & Begin Arc:

10. Moving on the balls of your feet, move both feet forward approximately 3 to 18 inches, utilizing a hopping/sliding motion. As you are completing the hop/slide forward, you will begin to execute the kick.

11. Using the toes of your kicking foot, while simultaneously pivoting approximately 45-degrees (counterclockwise) on the ball of your base leg foot, push off the floor and bring your kicking leg up and across the front of your body at approximately a 45-degree angle to your opponents right. Your leg should be straight, and your kicking foot should already be in the correct position to strike your opponent.

12. As your bring your kicking leg up, your upper body

Hop/Slide Forward & Begin Arc Foot Position

Hop/Slide Forward &... Front View

Hop/Slide Forward &... Side View

should now be facing at a slight angle toward your opponent and leaning back slightly. In this position, the kicking leg side of your body will be closer to your opponent than your base leg side. Your back will remain straight but not rigid.

13. Although your hands have switched position, they should still be held up (like a boxer's), with the elbows tucked in to protect the ribs and your hands up to protect your head.

14. Your head is up and facing towards your opponent, while your eyes remain in contact with your opponent throughout the entire kick.

Peak of Arc:

15. Your base leg foot should now have moved approximately 45-degrees counterclockwise by pivoting on the ball of your foot, while the knee on your base leg remains slightly bent. Your kicking leg has now moved up to your opponent's head height, although still at a 45-degree angle to your opponents right.

Peak of Arc Foot Position

16. Your kicking foot remains in the correct striking position throughout the entire sequence.

17. Your upper body, with the kicking leg side of your body remaining closer to your opponent than your base leg side, should still be facing at approximately a 45-degree angle to the right of your opponent, while continuing to lean back slightly.

18. Your head should still be up and facing towards your opponent, while your eyes continue to remain in contact with your opponent throughout the entire kick.

Peak of Arc Front View   *Peak of Arc Side View*

102

Impact:

19. Your base leg foot should now have moved approximately another 30-degrees (clockwise) by pivoting on the ball of your foot. At the moment of impact, your entire base leg foot should be in contact with the ground and gripping it.

*Impact
Foot Position*

20. Your upper body, with the kicking leg side of your body remaining closer to your opponent than your base leg side, should now be facing almost directly at your opponent, while continuing to lean back slightly. At the moment of impact, your entire body should tighten to add power to the kick, as your foot continues to travel on a straight and level "Path of Trajectory" through the target.

21. Notice how your kicking foot, kicking leg, hips, back, shoulders, and head are all in alignment at the initial moment of "Impact." Also, notice how the toes of the kicking foot are pulled back towards your body and pointed up. This helps insure that contact with the target is made with the outside edge of your heel, not your ankle!

22. Your head should still be facing towards your opponent. Eye contact with your opponent is maintained at all times.

Note: Another mistake that is quite common with martial artists, is to kick too high and go over their opponent's head. Don't kick over your opponent's head, <u>kick through your opponent's head!</u>

Impact Front View

Impact Side View

Follow Through:

23. Depending on your foot position during "Impact," your base leg foot will either continue to pivot approximately 30-degrees clockwise, or it will remain in contact with the ground and gripping it, while in approximately the same position it was in during "Impact." In either case, the knee on your base leg will remain slightly bent.

Follow Through
Foot Position

24. Your upper body is now facing directly towards your opponent and leaning back slightly. Although your body is in this position, your back will remain straight but not rigid.

25. Your kicking leg foot should continue along exactly the same straight and level path it followed from the "Peak of Arc" to "Impact." Your foot should still remain at your opponent's head height, although it should now be at a 45-degree angle to your opponents left.

26. Your head should still be facing towards your opponent. Eye contact with your opponent is maintained at all times.

Note: One of the inherit dangers of executing a Reverse Crescent Kick is the possibility of your kicking leg getting stuck up on top of your opponent's shoulder, or your opponent grabbing your kicking leg. Therefore, it is imperative that you practice retracting your leg from this precarious position by bringing your knee to your chest and then recoiling your kicking foot as if you had just executed a Front Kick.

Follow Through Front View   *Follow Through Side View*

End of Arc:

27. Once again, depending on your foot position during the "Impact" phase of the kick, your base leg foot will continue to pivot anywhere from 30 to 90-degrees clockwise. Regardless of how far your base leg continues to pivot, the knee on your base leg will remain slightly bent.

28. Your kicking leg remains straight with the knee slightly bent. Your kicking foot is now at approximately a 45-degree angle to your right (your opponent's left), at approximately the height of your base leg knee.

29. Your upper body, with the base leg side of your body now closer to your opponent than your kicking leg side, should now be facing at approximately a 45-degree angle to the left of your opponent, although you should no longer be leaning back. Your back should be straight, but not rigid.

30. Your head should still be up with your eyes looking directly at your opponent, whether he is still standing, or lying on the ground.

End of Arc
Foot Position

Note: The kicking motion of the Back Leg Reverse Crescent Kick is the exact opposite of the Back Leg Crescent Kick, which is the primary kick discussed in great detail in Volume Four.

End of Arc Front View   *End of Arc Side View*

Return to Fighting Position:

There are two ways that you can return to a fighting position from the "End of Arc" position. They are as follows:

31a. After you have reached the "End of Arc" position, simply bring your kicking foot behind you and set it down into a fighting position with your kicking leg behind you, rather than in front of you.

Position #1

31b. After you have reached the "End of Arc" position, simply leave your kicking foot in front of you and set it down into a fighting position with your kicking leg in front of you, rather than behind you.

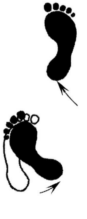 

Position #2

Note: The front view of a Reverse Crescent Kick can also be compared to a wagon wheel, which is shown here on the right. The hub or center or the wagon wheel is representative of your hips, while your kicking leg is represented by the spokes in the wagon wheel and your kicking foot is represented by the outer rim.

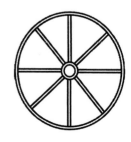

Pictorial Overview:

Fighting Position

Hop/Slide Forward &...

Begin Arc

Peak of Arc

Impact

FollowThrough

End of Arc

Position #1

Position #2

107

Hop/Slide Backward Reverse Crescent Kick

The Hopping/Sliding Backward Reverse Crescent Kick is identical in execution to the Back Leg Reverse Crescent Kick, with one notable exception. A hopping/sliding backward motion, which is performed immediately prior to executing the kick. This hopping/sliding backward motion is used to draw your opponent into you, or to avoid an attack. It can also increase the power in this kick due to the added momentum of hopping/sliding backward. The actual hop or slide motion is performed by both feet simultaneously moving backward keeping the same distance between them. The hop or slide can be anywhere from a few inches up to 18 inches. Keep your hips and upper body as still as possible throughout the initial hop or slide backward in order to avoid telegraphing the move to your opponent.

Fighting Position:

1. Your fighting position for this kick is exactly the same as it was for Back Leg Reverse Crescent Kick. With your kicking leg in the rearward position to begin with rather than in the forward position.
2. This stance is approximately shoulder width apart with the heel of your rear foot in a direct line with the heel of your front foot.
3. Your front or lead foot should be pointing directly at your opponent.
4. Your rear foot is angled toward the right at approximately a 45-degree angle. Your weight should be distributed evenly over the balls of both feet.
5. Your knees are slightly, but not noticeably bent. They should not be locked straight or rigid.

Fighting Position
Foot Position

Fighting Position Front View

Hop/Slide
Backward

Fighting Position Side View

6. Your body should be facing at a 45-degree angle toward your opponent. This presents a smaller target area and also facilitates a faster hop/slide backward, which allows you the opportunity to initiate a faster kick.

7. Your hands should be held up (like a boxers), with the elbows tucked in to protect the ribs and your hands up to protect your head. Your hands should remain as close to this position as possible throughout the entire kick.

8. Your head should be facing your opponent with your chin tucked down and protected by your lead shoulder.

9. Your eyes should be centered on your opponent's chest.

Hop/Slide Backward & Begin Arc:

10. Moving on the balls of your feet, move both feet backward approximately 3 to 18 inches, utilizing a hopping/sliding motion. As you are completing the hop/slide backward, you will begin to execute the kick.

11. Using the toes of your kicking foot, while simultaneously pivoting approximately 45-degrees (counterclockwise) on the ball of your base leg foot, push off the floor and bring your kicking leg up and across the front of your body and at approximately a 45-degree angle to your opponents right. Your leg should be straight, and your kicking foot should already be in the correct position to strike your opponent.

12. As your bring your kicking leg up, your upper body

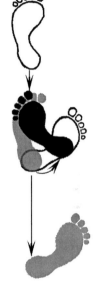

*Hop/Slide Backward
& Begin Arc
Foot Position*

Hop/Slide Back & Begin Arc Front View   *Hop/Slide Back & Begin Arc Side View*

should now be facing at a slight angle toward your opponent and leaning back slightly. In this position, the kicking leg side of your body will be closer to your opponent than your base leg side. Your back will remain straight but not rigid.

13. Although your hands have switched position, they should still be held up (like a boxer's), with the elbows tucked in to protect the ribs and your hands up to protect your head.

14. Your head is up and facing towards your opponent, while your eyes remain in contact with your opponent throughout the entire kick.

Peak of Arc:

15. Your base leg foot should now have moved approximately 45-degrees counterclockwise by pivoting on the ball of your foot, while the knee on your base leg remains slightly bent. Your kicking leg has now moved up to your opponent's head height, although still at a 45-degree angle to your opponents right.

Peak of Arc Foot Position

16. Your kicking foot remains in the correct striking position throughout the entire sequence.

17. Your upper body, with the kicking leg side of your body remaining closer to your opponent than your base leg side, should still be facing at approximately a 45-degree angle to the right of your opponent, while continuing to lean back slightly.

18. Your head should still be up and facing towards your opponent, while your eyes continue to remain in contact with your opponent throughout the entire kick.

Peak of Arc Front View   *Peak of Arc Side View*

Impact:

19. Your base leg foot should now have moved approximately another 30-degrees (clockwise) by pivoting on the ball of your foot. At the moment of impact, your entire base leg foot should be in contact with the ground and gripping it.

Impact
Foot Position

20. Your upper body, with the kicking leg side of your body remaining closer to your opponent than your base leg side, should now be facing almost directly at your opponent, while continuing to lean back slightly. At the moment of impact, your entire body should tighten to add power to the kick, as your foot continues to travel on a straight and level "Path of Trajectory" through the target.

21. Notice how your kicking foot, kicking leg, hips, back, shoulders, and head are all in alignment at the initial moment of "Impact." Also, notice how the toes of the kicking foot are pulled back towards your body and pointed up. This helps insure that contact with the target is made with the outside edge of your heel, not your ankle!

22. Your head should still be facing towards your opponent. Eye contact with your opponent is maintained at all times.

Note: For optimum results upon impact, you must use a combination of proper technique, along with an explosive combination of speed and strength.

Impact Front View

Impact Side View

Follow Through:

23. Depending on your foot position during "Impact," your base leg foot will either continue to pivot approximately 30-degrees clockwise, or it will remain in contact with the ground and gripping it, while in approximately the same position it was in during "Impact." In either case, the knee on your base leg will remain slightly bent.

Follow Through Foot Position

24. Your upper body is now facing directly towards your opponent and leaning back slightly. Although your body is in this position, your back will remain straight but not rigid.

25. Your kicking leg foot should continue along exactly the same straight and level path it followed from the "Peak of Arc" to "Impact." Your foot should still remain at your opponent's head height, although it should now be at a 45-degree angle to your opponents left.

26. Your head should still be facing towards your opponent. Eye contact with your opponent is maintained at all times.

Note: Utilize proper footwork prior to executing your kick in order to get the optimum kicking range between you and your opponent. If you are to far away, you will not hit your target. If you are to close, you will "jam" your own kick. Either one of these is ineffective and has the potential to leave you in a very dangerous position.

Follow Through Front View   *Follow Through Side View*

End of Arc:

27. Once again, depending on your foot position during the "Impact" phase of the kick, your base leg foot will continue to pivot anywhere from 30 to 90-degrees clockwise. Regardless of how far your base leg continues to pivot, the knee on your base leg will remain slightly bent.

*End of Arc
Foot Position*

28. Your kicking leg remains straight with the knee slightly bent. Your kicking foot is now at approximately a 45-degree angle to your right (your opponent's left), at approximately the height of your base leg knee.

29. Your upper body, with the base leg side of your body now closer to your opponent than your kicking leg side, should now be facing at approximately a 45-degree angle to the left of your opponent, although you should no longer be leaning back. Your back should be straight, but not rigid.

30. Your head should still be up with your eyes looking directly at your opponent, whether he is still standing, or lying on the ground.

Note: Throughout the entire kicking sequence, you can see that my arms are held up and close to my body, they are not flapping around like a bird. If you find yourself doing this, remember that it is incorrect and a quite common mistake that many martial artists make when kicking. Remember to keep your arms up and close to your body.

End of Arc Front View   *End of Arc Side View*

Return to Fighting Position:

There are two ways that you can return to a fighting position from the "End of Arc" position. They are as follows:

31a. After you have reached the "End of Arc" position, simply bring your kicking foot behind you and set it down into a fighting position with your kicking leg behind you, rather than in front of you.

Position #1

31b. After you have reached the "End of Arc" position, simply leave your kicking foot in front of you and set it down into a fighting position with your kicking leg in front of you, rather than behind you.

Position #2

Note: Once you become proficient executing the Hop/Slide Forward Reverse Crescent Kick and the Hop/Slide Backward Reverse Crescent Kick, you will want to strike your target just after your base leg foot ends its hop/slide forward, or its hop/slide backward. Remember that all of these kicks should eventually be executed in one fluid motion. However, one must first learn how to execute each stage of the kick correctly before putting it all together. TAKE YOUR TIME!

Pictorial Overview:

Fighting Position

Hop/Slide Backward &...

Begin Arc

Peak of Arc

Impact

FollowThrough

End of Arc

Position #1

Position #2

115

Front Leg Reverse Crescent Kick

The Front Leg Reverse Crescent Kick is identical in execution to the Back Leg Reverse Crescent Kick, with one notable exception. Instead of kicking with the rear leg, you are going to kick with your front leg. This kick is executed by shifting your weight onto your rear leg while bringing your front leg up and across your body at a 45-degree angle to your opponent's right into the "Begin Arc" phase of the kick. Although this is perhaps the weakest of all the Reverse Crescent Kicks in this book, it is still a necessary and very effective kick. With practice, this can be one of the fastest Reverse Crescent Kicks in your kicking arsenal.

Fighting Position:

1. Your fighting position for this kick is exactly the same as it was for Spinning Reverse Crescent Kick. With your kicking leg in the forward position to begin with rather than in the rearward position.
2. This stance is approximately shoulder width apart with the heel of your rear foot in a direct line with the heel of your front foot.
3. Your front or lead foot should be pointing directly at your opponent.
4. Your rear foot is angled toward the left at approximately a 45-degree angle. Your weight should be distributed evenly over the balls of both feet.
5. Your knees are slightly, but not noticeably bent. They should not be locked straight or rigid.
6. Your body should be facing at a 45-degree angle toward

*Fighting Position
Foot Position*

Fighting Position Front View

Fighting Position Side View

your opponent. This presents a smaller target area and also allows you the opportunity to initiate a faster kick.

7. Your hands should be held up (like a boxers), with the elbows tucked in to protect the ribs and your hands up to protect your head. Your hands should remain as close to this position as possible throughout the entire kick.

8. Your head should be facing your opponent with your chin tucked down and protected by your lead shoulder.

9. Your eyes should be centered on your opponent's chest.

Begin Arc:

10. Using the toes of your kicking foot, push off the floor and bring your kicking leg up and across your body at approximately a 45-degree angle to your opponents right. Your leg should be straight, and your kicking foot should already be in the correct position to strike your opponent.

11. As your bring your kicking leg up, your upper body should start turning as it begins to face towards your opponent. Your back will remain straight but not rigid.

12. Although your hands have switched position, they should still be held up (like a boxer's), with the elbows tucked in to protect the ribs and your hands up to protect your head.

Begin Arc Foot Position

13. Your head is up and facing towards your opponent, while your eyes remain in contact with your opponent throughout the entire kick.

Begin Arc Front View   *Begin Arc Side View*

117

Peak of Arc:

14. Your base leg foot should now have moved approximately 45-degrees counterclockwise by pivoting on the ball of your foot, while the knee on your base leg remains slightly bent. Your kicking leg has now moved up to your opponent's head height, although still at a 45-degree angle to your opponents right.

Peak of Arc
Foot Position

15. Your kicking foot remains in the correct striking position throughout the entire sequence.

16. Your upper body, with the kicking leg side of your body remaining closer to your opponent than your base leg side, continues to move in a clockwise direction and should be facing at approximately a 45-degree angle to the right of your opponent, while continuing to lean back slightly.

17. Your head should still be up and facing towards your opponent, while your eyes continue to remain in contact with your opponent throughout the entire kick.

Note: If your opponent is too far away from you, you can use footwork to adjust the distance between you and your opponent simply by moving your rearward foot closer to your lead foot prior to executing the kick.

Peak of Arc Front View   *Peak of Arc Side View*

Impact:

18. Your base leg foot should now have moved approximately 30-degrees (clockwise) by pivoting on the ball of your foot. At the moment of impact, your entire base leg foot should be in contact with the ground and gripping it.

Impact Foot Position

19. Your upper body, with the kicking leg side of your body remaining closer to your opponent than your base leg side, should now be facing almost directly at your opponent, while continuing to lean back slightly. At the moment of impact, your entire body should tighten to add power to the kick, as your foot continues to travel on a straight and level "Path of Trajectory" through the target.

20. Notice how your kicking foot, kicking leg, hips, back, shoulders, and head are all in alignment at the initial moment of "Impact." Also, notice how the toes of the kicking foot are pulled back towards your body and pointed up. This helps insure that contact with the target is made with the outside edge of your heel, not your ankle!

21. Your head should still be facing towards your opponent. Eye contact with your opponent is maintained at all times.

Note: You must learn to control the body's innate response to pull back or slow down when it is about to impact with something.

Impact Front View

Impact Side View

Follow Through:

22. Depending on your foot position during "Impact," your base leg foot will either continue to pivot approximately 30-degrees clockwise, or it will remain in contact with the ground and gripping it, while in approximately the same position it was in during "Impact." In either case, the knee on your base leg will remain slightly bent.

Follow Through Foot Position

23. Your upper body is now facing directly towards your opponent and leaning back slightly. Although your body is in this position, your back will remain straight but not rigid.

24. Your kicking leg foot should continue along exactly the same straight and level path it followed from the "Peak of Arc" to "Impact." Your foot should still remain at your opponent's head height, although it should now be at a 45-degree angle to your opponents left.

25. Your head should still be facing towards your opponent. Eye contact with your opponent is maintained at all times.

Incorrect

Correct

Follow Through Front View

Follow Through Side View

End of Arc:

26. Once again, depending on your foot position during the "Impact" phase of the kick, your base leg foot will continue to pivot anywhere from 30 to 90-degrees clockwise. Regardless of how far your base leg continues to pivot, the knee on your base leg will remain slightly bent.

End of Arc
Foot Position

27. Your kicking leg remains straight with the knee slightly bent. Your kicking foot is now at approximately a 45-degree angle to your right (your opponent's left), at approximately the height of your base leg knee.

28. Your upper body, with the base leg side of your body now closer to your opponent than your kicking leg side, should now be facing at approximately a 45-degree angle to the left of your opponent, although you should no longer be leaning back. Your back should be straight, but not rigid.

29. Your head should still be up with your eyes looking directly at your opponent, whether he is still standing, or lying on the ground.

Note: Whether or not you are kicking to the body or head, the same principle of <u>STRIKING THROUGH</u> the target applies. However, you must keep in mind that the head moves a lot easier than the body, is farther from the ground than the body, and generally speaking, it takes longer for a kick to get from the ground to the head, than from the ground to the body.

End of Arc Front View   *End of Arc Side View*

Return to Fighting Position:

There are two ways that you can return to a fighting position from the "End of Arc" position. They are as follows:

30a. After you have reached the "End of Arc" position, simply bring your kicking foot behind you and set it down into a fighting position with your kicking leg behind you, rather than in front of you.

Position #1

30b. After you have reached the "End of Arc" position, simply leave your kicking foot in front of you and set it down into a fighting position with your kicking leg in front of you, rather than behind you.

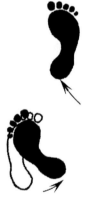

Position #2

Note: Although I have broken down all of the kicks in this book into various steps, you must remember that eventually you will be executing these kicks without thought in one fluid motion while adhering to every principle and technique described in this book in order to maximize the effectiveness of your kick.

Pictorial Overview:

Fighting Position   Begin Arc   Peak of Arc

Impact   FollowThrough   End of Arc

Position #1   Position #2

123

Cross-Over Reverse Crescent Kick

The Cross-Over Reverse Crescent Kick is identical in execution to the Back Leg Reverse Crescent Kick, with one notable exception. A cross-over forward motion, which is performed immediately prior to executing the kick. This motion is used to close the distance between you and your opponent, and also to misdirect or deceive your opponent in order to increase your chances of successfully executing the kick. It can also increase the power in this kick due to the added momentum of crossing-over forward. The actual cross-over motion is performed by stepping forward and across your lead foot with your rear foot, while your rear foot remains stationary except for a short counterclockwise pivot on the ball of the foot. The cross-over can be anywhere from a few inches to approximately your shoulder width. Keep your hips and upper body as still as possible throughout the initial cross-over in order to avoid telegraphing the move to your opponent.

Fighting Position:

1. Your fighting position for this kick is exactly the same as it was for Step-Back Reverse Crescent Kick. With your kicking leg in the forward position to begin with rather than in the rearward position.
2. This stance is approximately shoulder width apart with the heel of your rear foot in a direct line with the heel of your front foot.
3. Your front or lead foot should be pointing directly at your opponent.
4. Your rear foot is angled toward the left at approximately a 45-degree angle. Your weight should be distributed evenly

Fighting Position Foot Position

Fighting Position Front View

Cross-Over

Fighting Position Side View

over the balls of both feet.

5. Your knees are slightly, but not noticeably bent. They should not be locked straight or rigid.
6. Your body should be facing at a 45-degree angle toward your opponent. This presents a smaller target area and also facilitates a faster cross-over, which allows you the opportunity to initiate a faster kick.
7. Your hands should be held up (like a boxers), with the elbows tucked in to protect the ribs and your hands up to protect your head. Your hands should remain as close to this position as possible throughout the entire kick.
8. Your head should be facing your opponent with your chin tucked down and protected by your lead shoulder.
9. Your eyes should be centered on your opponent's chest.

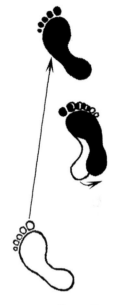

Cross-Over:

10. Keeping your upper body and hips as still as possible, step forward and across the front of your lead leg foot with your rear leg foot. When you place your rear foot back down on the ground, it should be angled toward the left at approximately a 45-degree angle. As soon as the ball of your rear foot touches the ground, begin to execute the kick.

Cross-Over
Foot Position

Cross-Over Front View   *Cross-Over Side View*

125

Begin Arc:

11. Using the toes of your kicking foot, push off the floor and bring your kicking leg up at approximately a 45-degree angle. Your leg should be straight, and your kicking foot should already be in the correct position to strike your opponent.

12. As your bring your kicking leg up, your upper body should remain facing at approximately a 45-degree angle to the right of your opponent. Your back will remain straight, but not rigid.

13. Although your hands have switched position, they should still be held up (like a boxer's), with the elbows tucked in to protect the ribs and your hands up to protect your head.

14. Your head is up and facing towards your opponent, while your eyes continue to remain in contact with your opponent throughout the entire kick.

Begin Arc
Foot Position

Note: As I explained to you on page 26, and have illustrated for you on the following page, if you apply the correct surface area to the correct target, it is like driving a nail into a board. If however, you strike the target incorrectly without applying all of the proper principles and correct techniques, your effectiveness will be greatly reduced and you may cause more damage to yourself rather than your opponent.

Begin Arc Front View   *Begin Arc Side View*

Peak of Arc:

15. Your base leg foot should now have moved approximately 45-degrees counterclockwise by pivoting on the ball of your foot, while the knee on your base leg remains slightly bent. Your kicking leg has now moved up to your opponent's head height, although still at a 45-degree angle to your opponents right.

16. Your kicking foot remains in the correct striking position throughout the entire sequence.

17. Your upper body, with the kicking leg side of your body remaining closer to your opponent than your base leg side, should still be facing at approximately a 45-degree angle to the right of your opponent, while continuing to lean back slightly.

18. Your head should still be up and facing towards your opponent, while your eyes continue to remain in contact with your opponent throughout the entire kick.

*Peak of Arc
Foot Position*

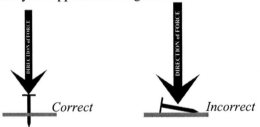

Correct   *Incorrect*   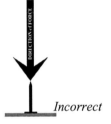 *Incorrect*

Peak of Arc Front View   *Peak of Arc Side View*

Impact:

19. Your base leg foot should now have moved approximately another 30-degrees (clockwise) by pivoting on the ball of your foot. At the moment of impact, your entire base leg foot should be in contact with the ground and gripping it.

20. Your upper body, with the kicking leg side of your body remaining closer to your opponent than your base leg side, should now be facing almost directly at your opponent, while continuing to lean back slightly. At the moment of impact, your entire body should tighten to add power to the kick, as your foot continues to travel on a straight and level "Path of Trajectory" through the target.

Impact
Foot Position

21. Notice how your kicking foot, kicking leg, hips, back, shoulders, and head are all in alignment at the initial moment of "Impact." Also, notice how the toes of the kicking foot are pulled back towards your body and pointed up. This helps insure that contact with the target is made with the outside edge of your heel, not your ankle!

22. Your head should still be facing towards your opponent. Eye contact with your opponent is maintained at all times.

Note: Look closely at the photographs below, see how vulnerable you are in this position? Constantly strive to kick faster than you can blink!

Impact Front View   *Impact Side View*

Follow Through:

23. Depending on your foot position during "Impact," your base leg foot will either continue to pivot approximately 30-degrees clockwise, or it will remain in contact with the ground and gripping it, while in approximately the same position it was in during "Impact." In either case, the knee on your base leg will remain slightly bent.

Follow Through
Foot Position

24. Your upper body is now facing directly towards your opponent and leaning back slightly. Although your body is in this position, your back will remain straight but not rigid.

25. Your kicking leg foot should continue along exactly the same straight and level path it followed from the "Peak of Arc" to "Impact." Your foot should still remain at your opponent's head height, although it should now be at a 45-degree angle to your opponents left.

26. Your head should still be facing towards your opponent. Eye contact with your opponent is maintained at all times.

Note: In order to generate the maximum amount of power possible when executing not only the Reverse Crescent Kick, but any kick, punch or strike, you must adhere to the correct execution of movement throughout the entire kicking sequence. Just as in boxing, power must first be generated by the movement of the feet, legs, hips, body, and shoulders prior to <u>STRIKING THROUGH</u> your target.

Follow Through Front View

Follow Through Side View

End of Arc:

27. Once again, depending on your foot position during the "Impact" phase of the kick, your base leg foot will continue to pivot anywhere from 30 to 90-degrees clockwise. Regardless of how far your base leg continues to pivot, the knee on your base leg will remain slightly bent.

28. Your kicking leg remains straight with the knee slightly bent. Your kicking foot is now at approximately a 45-degree angle to your right (your opponent's left), at approximately the height of your base leg knee.

29. Your upper body, with the base leg side of your body now closer to your opponent than your kicking leg side, should now be facing at approximately a 45-degree angle to the left of your opponent, although you should no longer be leaning back. Your back should be straight, but not rigid.

30. Your head should still be up with your eyes looking directly at your opponent, whether he is still standing, or lying on the ground.

End of Arc
Foot Position

Note: Would you chop down a tree with a tennis racket? Would you hit a tennis ball with an axe? Remember to use the correct tool for each particular situation. Kicking may be effective in one situation, but ineffective in another. A Reverse Crescent Kick may be the correct kick to use in one kicking situation, but totally ineffective in another.

End of Arc Front View   *End of Arc Side View*

Return to Fighting Position:

There are two ways that you can return to a fighting position from the "End of Arc" position. They are as follows:

31a. After you have reached the "End of Arc" position, simply bring your kicking foot behind you and set it down into a fighting position with your kicking leg behind you, rather than in front of you.

Position #1

31b. After you have reached the "End of Arc" position, simply leave your kicking foot in front of you and set it down into a fighting position with your kicking leg in front of you, rather than behind you.

Position #2

Note: Not only does following the correct upward "Path of Trajectory" by utilizing a big arcing motion create more power, but it also allows you to avoid having your kicking leg grabbed by your opponent and/or your kicking leg blocked by your opponent's legs. Always remember, the shortest distance between point A and point B may not always be the quickest, safest, or most efficient.

Pictorial Overview:

Fighting Position   Corss-Over   Begin Arc

Peak of Arc   Impact   FollowThrough

End of Arc   Position #1   Position #2

Off-Setting Turning Reverse Crescent Kick

The Off-Setting Turning Reverse Crescent Kick is identical in execution to the Turning Reverse Crescent Kick, with one notable exception. A quick double step motion to the side (putting you at a 45-degree angle from your original starting position), which is performed immediately prior to executing the kick. The starting position is the same as Turning Reverse Crescent Kick, in that your kicking foot is in the rearward position rather than the forward position. The actual double-step motion of the feet prior to the execution of the kick is performed by first moving the rearward foot and then the forward foot off at a 45-degree angle to the side of your opponent. When executing the double-step motion, be sure and move your rearward foot first, then your forward foot, without initially moving your hips and upper body in order to avoid telegraphing the move to your opponent. Your hips and upper body will begin to move when you begin to place the forward foot back onto the ground.

Fighting Position:

1. Your fighting position for this kick is the exact same as Turning Reverse Crescent Kick, in that your kicking leg will be in the rearward position to begin with rather than in the forward position.

2. This stance is approximately shoulder width apart with the heel of your rear foot directly in line with the heel of your front foot

3. Your front or lead foot should be pointed directly at your opponent.

4. Your rear foot is angled toward the right at approximately a 45-degree angle. Your weight should be distributed evenly over the balls of both feet.

Fighting Position Foot Position

5. Your knees are slightly, but not noticeably bent. They

Fighting Position Front View

Fighting Position Side View

133

should not be locked straight or rigid.

6. Your body should be facing at a 45-degree angle towards your opponent. This presents a smaller target area and also facilitates a faster off-set and turn, which allows you the opportunity to initiate a faster kick.

7. Your hands should be held up (like a boxer's), with the elbows tucked in to protect the ribs and your hands up to protect your head. Your hands should remain as close to this position as possible throughout the entire kick.

8. Your head should be facing your opponent with your chin tucked down and protected by your lead shoulder.

9. Your eyes should be centered on your opponent's chest.

Off-Set (part one):

10. Move your rear foot to the right (approximately 2-3 feet), and slightly forward (approximately 8 to 10 inches).

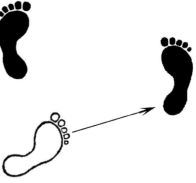

Off-Set Foot Position (part one)

First Step on Off-Set Front View

First Step on Off-Set Side View

Off-Set (part two) & Turn:

11. Move your front foot to the right approximately 12 to 18 inches. While moving your front foot, pivot on the ball of your rear foot. This will turn your back towards your opponent. As you set your front foot down, the heel of your front foot should now be fac-

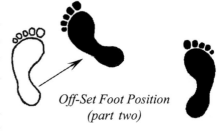

Off-Set Foot Position (part two)

ing towards your opponent. However, when first learning this kick, make the off-setting and the turn two separate moves.

12. Your body should now be at a 45 -degree angle from its original starting position, and you should be ready to execute a Turning Reverse Crescent Kick.

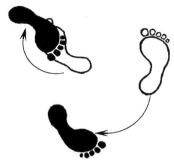

Turning Foot Position

Second Step on Off-Set Front View

Second Step on Off-Set Side View

Turning Front View

Turning Side View

Begin Arc:

13. Using the toes of your kicking foot, push off the floor and bring your kicking leg up at approximately a 45-degree angle. Your leg should be straight, and your kicking foot should already be in the correct position to strike your opponent.

14. As your bring your kicking leg up, your upper body should continue turning 360-degrees clockwise as it begins to face towards your opponent. Your back will remain straight, but not rigid.

15. Although your hands have switched position, they should still be held up (like a boxer's), with the elbows tucked in to protect the ribs and your hands up to protect your head.

16. Your head is up and facing towards your opponent, while your eyes continue to remain in contact with your opponent throughout the entire kick.

Begin Arc
Foot Position

Note: The ability to effectively and efficiently utilize high section kicks depends primarily on the following four factors. A: Your expertise in kicking. B: Your overall flexibility and physical condition. C: Your environment at the time. D: Your opponent.

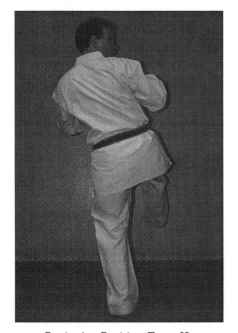

Begin Arc Position Front View   *Begin Arc Position Side View*

Peak of Arc:

17. Your base leg foot should now have moved approximately 45-degrees clockwise by pivoting on the ball of your foot, while the knee on your base leg remains slightly bent. Your kicking leg has now moved up to your opponent's head height, although still at a 45-degree angle to your opponents front.

Peak of Arc
Foot Position

18. Your kicking foot remains in the correct striking position throughout the entire sequence.

19. Your upper body, with the kicking leg side of your body remaining closer to your opponent than your base leg side, continues to move in a clockwise direction and should be facing at approximately a 45-degree angle to the front of your opponent, while continuing to lean back slightly.

20. Your head should still be up and facing towards your opponent, while your eyes continue to remain in contact with your opponent throughout the entire kick.

Note: The "Off-Setting" movement is one of the primary techniques utilized in the "8 Directions of Attack" strategy. This is a very important strategic technique and one that can be utilized in any martial art.

Peak of Arc Front View   *Peak of Arc Side View*

Impact:

21. Your base leg foot should now have moved approximately another 45-degrees (clockwise) by pivoting on the ball of your foot. At the moment of impact, your entire base leg foot should be in contact with the ground and gripping it.

Impact
Foot Position

22. Your upper body, with the kicking leg side of your body remaining closer to your opponent than your base leg side, should now be facing almost directly at your opponent, while continuing to lean back slightly. At the moment of impact, your entire body should tighten to add power to the kick, as your foot continues to travel on a straight and level "Path of Trajectory" through the target.

23. Notice how your kicking foot, kicking leg, hips, back, shoulders, and head are all in alignment at the initial moment of "Impact." Also, notice how the toes of the kicking foot are pulled back towards your body and pointed up. This helps insure that contact with the target is made with the outside edge of your heel, not your ankle!

24. Your head should still be facing towards your opponent. Eye contact with your opponent is maintained at all times.

Note: When properly applied, the footwork motion of off-setting prior to kicking can greatly increase the power generated in a Turning Reverse Crescent Kick.

Impact Front View

Impact Side View

Follow Through:

25. Depending on your foot position during "Impact," your base leg foot will either continue to pivot approximately 30-degrees clockwise, or it will remain in contact with the ground and gripping it, while in approximately the same position it was in during "Impact." In either case, the knee on your base leg will remain slightly bent.

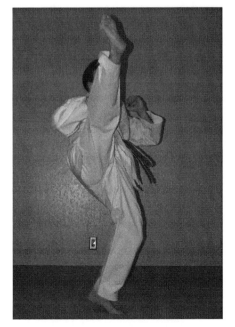

Follow Through Foot Position

26. Your upper body is now facing directly towards your opponent and leaning back slightly. Although your body is in this position, your back will remain straight but not rigid.

27. Your kicking leg foot should continue along exactly the same straight and level path it followed from the "Peak of Arc" to "Impact." Your foot should still remain at your opponent's head height, although it should now be at a 45-degree angle to to the rear of your opponent.

28. Your head should still be facing towards your opponent. Eye contact with your opponent is maintained at all times.

Note: The primary reason that martial artists injure their knees when kicking, is due to improper pivoting on the base leg foot. Always pivot on the ball of your foot, not the heel.

Follow Through Front View

Follow Through Side View

End of Arc:

29. Once again, depending on your foot position during the "Impact" phase of the kick, your base leg foot will continue to pivot anywhere from 30 to 90-degrees clockwise. Regardless of how far your base leg continues to pivot, the knee on your base leg will remain slightly bent.

30. Your kicking leg remains straight with the knee slightly bent. Your kicking foot is now at approximately a 45-degree angle to your right (your opponent's left), at approximately the height of your base leg knee.

31. Your upper body, with the base leg side of your body now closer to your opponent than your kicking leg side, should now be facing at approximately a 45-degree angle to the rear of your opponent, although you should no longer be leaning back. Your back should be straight, but not rigid.

32. Your head should still be up with your eyes looking directly at your opponent, whether he is still standing, or lying on the ground.

*End of Arc
Foot Position*

Note: Your first line of defense should be your kicks, as they are your longest and most powerful weapons in your arsenal. Kicking falls into the "Long Range" category, while punching and hand strikes fall into the "Mid Range" category. Knee and elbow strikes fall into the "Short Range" category, while joint techniques fall into your final range, Grappling."

End of Arc Front View

End of Arc Side View

Return to Fighting Position:

33. Your entire body from your head to your toes, continues the 360-degree clockwise motion and should now be in exactly the same fighting position that you were in prior to executing this kick.

34. Your kicking leg foot also continues the 360-degree clockwise motion and returns to its original starting position. Your kicking leg knee will remain slightly bent as it returns to the starting position.

35. Your hands, which should have remained as close to this position as possible throughout the entire kick, are held up (like a boxer's), with the elbows tucked in to protect the ribs and your hands up to protect your head.

36. Your head should now be looking over your lead leg shoulder with your eyes in contact with your opponent.

Return to Fighting Position Foot Position

Note: You should now be in the exact same position that you were in, after executing the initial off-setting movement.

Note: If you want to learn how to improve your strategic thinking, learn not only how to play the game of chess, but also how to study the game of chess.

Return to Fighting Position Front View

Return to Fighting Position Side View

141

Pictorial Overview:

Fighting Position   Off-Set (part one)   Off-Set (part two)

Turn   Begin Arc   Peak of Arc

Impact   Follow Through   End of Arc

Return to Fighting Position

Note: Occasionally when executing a Reverse Crescent Kick, you will find that your kicking foot will not be able to "Follow Through" after impacting with the appropriate vital or vulnerable point on your opponent. Usually, what will end up happening is either your leg just stops, or a "bouncing" effect that will take place immediately after initial impact with your opponent. This takes the form of your leg "bouncing" back towards the "Peak of Arc" position after striking your opponent rather than going through your opponent. If and when either of these two things happen, do not try and force your kicking foot through the target. Instead, go with the "bounce" and retract your kicking leg immediately by bringing your knee toward your chest while simultaneously bringing your kicking foot back toward your body by bending your kicking leg knee. Just like recoiling or retracting your kicking leg after executing a Front Kick.

Jump Turning Reverse Crescent Kick

The Jump Turning Reverse Crescent Kick is identical in execution to the Turning Reverse Crescent Kick, with one notable exception. That being a jumping motion that is performed immediately prior to executing the kick. This motion can be used to gain height in your kick, and it can also be used to gain distance either towards or away from your opponent. It can also increase the power in the kick due to the added momentum of jumping and then kicking. The actual jump turning motion is executed by bending your knees slightly and leaping either straight up, forward, or even backward depending on the situation and your opponent, in order to execute the kick. The jump itself should be practiced independently of the kick until you can execute the jump without telegraphing the kick by utilizing any unnecessary movements, such as hunching of the back and shoulders, bending of the knees too deeply, or winding up of the upper body. Remember that this is a jump turning kick, not a jump spinning one. There is a difference.

Fighting Position:

1. Your fighting position for this kick is the exact same as for a Turning Reverse Crescent Kick. That is your kicking leg will be in the rearward position to begin with rather than in the forward position.
2. This stance is approximately shoulder width apart with the heel of your rear foot in a direct line with the heel of your front foot.
3. Your front or lead foot should be pointed directly at your opponent.

Fighting Position
Foot Position

Fighting Position Front View

Fighting Position Side View

144

4. Your rear foot is angled towards the right at approximately a 45-degree angle. Your weight should be distributed evenly over the balls of both feet.

5. Your knees are slightly, but not noticeably bent. They should not be locked straight or rigid.

6. Your body should be facing at a 45-degree angle toward your opponent. This presents a smaller target area and also facilitates a faster jump and turn, which allows you the opportunity to initiate a faster kick

7. Your hands should be held up (like a boxer's), with the elbows tucked in to protect the ribs and your hands up to protect your head. Your hands should remain as close to this position as possible throughout the entire kick.

8. Your head should be facing your opponent with your chin tucked down and protected by your lead shoulder.

9. Your eyes should be centered on your opponent's chest.

Jump, Turn & Begin Arc:

10. Moving both feet simultaneously, jump straight up and begin turning your body in a clockwise motion. While you are in the air, the following things should be done simultaneously. They are as follows:

10a. Turn your head and look over your kicking shoulder. Eye contact with your opponent is maintained at all times.

10b. Bring your kicking leg up to the "Begin Arc" position.

10c. Keep your hands up throughout the entire kick.

10d. Your body, which should be straight but not rigid, should make a complete 360-degree turn while in the air. Execute the kick.

Jump, Turn & Begin Arc Front View   *Jump, Turn & Begin Arc Side View*

Peak of Arc:

11. Your kicking leg, with the knee slightly bent, has now moved up to the correct height to strike your target.
12. Even though you are in the air, the heel of your kicking foot should follow a straight line of trajectory from the "Peak of Arc" through the target (Impact), to the "Follow Through" position.
13. Your upper body should be straight, but not rigid.
14. Although your body is now in the above position. The front of your body should be at a 45-degree angle to the front of your opponent. While your back is facing at a 45-degree angle away from your opponent.
15. Your head should still be looking over your kicking leg shoulder. Eye contact with your target is maintained at all times.

Note: As you can see in the illustrations presented on the following page, the optimum angle for impact in relation to your opponent's head is a 90-degree angle. Therefore, the further away you are from a 90-degree angle, the less effective your kick is going to be. For example, as you look at the illustrations on the following page, imagine that you have not only an overhead view, but also a front view of your opponent's head. The black arrows are Reverse Crescent Kicks delivered to your opponent's jaw. Which one is going to be more effective, the one on the left? Or the one on the right?

Peak of Trajectory Front View   *Peak of Trajectory Side View*

146

Impact:

16. At the moment of impact, your entire body should tighten to add power to the kick. Notice how the toes of the kicking foot are pulled back towards your body and pointed up. This helps insure that contact with the target is made with the outside edge of the heel.
17. Your upper body should still be straight, but not rigid.
18. Notice how your body is now facing towards your opponent. However, it is at a slight angle due to the actions of the kicking leg and the continuous 360-degree turning motion of the entire body.
19. Your head should still be up and looking over your kicking leg shoulder. Eye contact with your target is maintained at all times.

Correct Angle of Attack
Top & Front View

Incorrect Angle of Attack
Top & Front View

Impact Front View

Impact Side View

Follow Through:

20. Your kicking foot should continue along exactly the same path it followed from the "Peak of Arc" to "Impact". Your foot should be approximately 45-degrees past your target.

21. Your upper body should still be upright and straight, but not rigid. The front of your body is now facing directly at the front of your opponent.

22. Your hands, which should have remained as close to the original starting position as possible, should still be up to protect your head and body. Did you notice my hand position in the "Front View" photograph? This is very incorrect!

23. Your head should no longer be looking over your kicking leg shoulder. However, your eyes are still looking at your opponent, not your kicking foot.

Note: When executing any Turning Reverse Crescent Kick, whether it is a ground based kick or an aerial kick, you want to have your body weight centered over the axis point of your 360-degree turn. Your axis point, will run in a straight "up and down" line from the ball of your base foot, through your base leg and up through your hips and upper body. If your weight is centered over your axis point, your body should "spin" just like the top which is pictured on the upper right, when you execute a 360-degree turn.

Follow Through Front View   *Follow Through Side View*

End of Arc:

24. Your base leg foot should have just touched down on the ground, and the toes of your base leg foot should now be pointing directly at your opponent.

25. Your kicking leg remains straight with the knee slightly bent. Your kicking foot is now slightly in front of you and to your right (your opponent's left), at approximately the height of your base leg knee.

26. Your upper body and back remain straight, but not rigid. While continuing to move clockwise, your upper body is now midway between facing directly at your opponent, and returning to its original fighting position at a 45-degree angle to your opponent.

27. Your head should still be up and looking directly over the center of your chest. Your eyes are still in contact with your opponent, whether he is still standing, or lying on the ground.

End of Trajectory
Foot Position

Note: However, if your weight is not centered over the axis point, say for example you have leaned to far back, then your "spin" will look more like a wobble, like the top which is pictured on the right, when you execute a 360-degree turn.

End of Trajectory Front View

End of Trajectory Side View

149

Return to Fighting Position:

28. Your entire body from your head to your toes, should be in exactly the same position that you initially started in (refer to the Fighting Position section of this kick), prior to executing this kick.

29. Your kicking leg foot continues the 360-degree motion and returns to its original starting position. Although your kicking leg knee will remain slightly bent as it returns to the starting position.

30. Your hands, which should have remained as close to this position as possible throughout the entire kick, are once again in the same position they were in prior to executing the kick.

31. Your head should now be looking over your lead leg shoulder with your eyes in contact with your opponent.

*Return to Fighting
Position
Foot Position*

Note: If you were to look at the basic outline of your body during the "Peak of Arc" through "Follow Through" phase of any Wheel Kick, it would have the basic appearance of a capital "Y". Which you can see in the much larger illustration on the right.

Return to Fighting Position Front View   *Return to Fighting Position Side View*

150

Pictorial Overview:

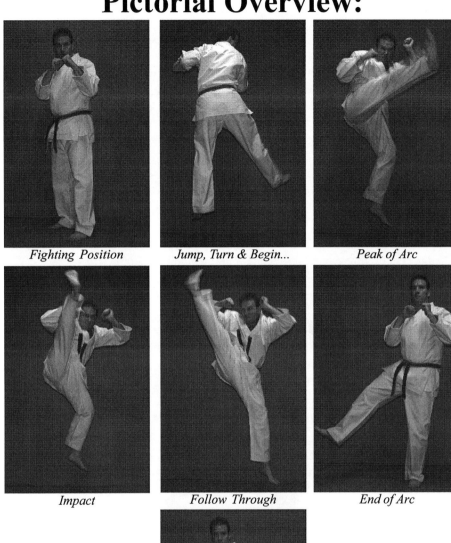

Fighting Position

Jump, Turn & Begin...

Peak of Arc

Impact

Follow Through

End of Arc

Return to Fighting Position

Switch Turning Reverse Crescent Kick
(With the left leg)

Here is an example on how to change the instructions presented in this book in order to execute the exact same kicks with the left leg. First of all you're going to be kicking with the left leg rather than the right, so your rear foot and body position will be exactly opposite of those that you would use if you were kicking with the right leg. To put it simply, kicking with the left leg should mirror exactly those kicks performed with the right leg and vice versa.

Fighting Position:

1. Your fighting position for this kick is the exact same as it was for Turning Reverse Crescent Kick. However, in this case, your kicking leg will be in the forward position to begin with rather than in the rearward position.

2. This stance is approximately shoulder width apart with the heel of your rear foot in a direct line with the heel of your front foot.

3. Your front or lead foot should be pointing directly at your opponent.

4. Your rear foot is angled towards the right at approximately a 45-degree angle. Your weight should be distributed evenlyover the balls of both feet.

5. Your knees are slightly, but not noticeably bent. They should not be locked or rigid.

6. Your body should be facing at a 45-degree angle toward

Fighting Position
Foot Position

Fighting Position Front View

Fighting Position Side View

152

your opponent. This presents a smaller target area and also facilitates a faster switch-and-turn, which allows you the opportunity to initiate a faster kick.

7. Your hands should be held up (like a boxer's), with the elbows tucked in to protect the ribs and your hands up to protect your head. Your hands should remain as close to this position as possible throughout the entire kick.

8. Your head should be facing your opponent with your chin tucked down and protected by your lead shoulder.

9. Your eyes should be centered on your opponents chest.

Switch Feet & Turn Back:

10. Utilizing a scissors type motion of your legs and feet, simultaneously switch your front foot with your rear foot. After you have begun the switching of the feet, turn your back towards your opponent. After switching, the heels of both of your feet should be pointed towards your opponent.

11. Prior to turning your back, your head should be turned over your kicking leg shoulder and your eyes should be looking at your opponent.

12. Your back should be facing directly toward your opponent.

*Switch Feet &
Turn Back
Foot Position*

Note: Utilize deception when fighting. Make sure your opponent believes that you are going to do one thing, when you really intend to do another.

Switch Feet & Turn Front View

Switch Feet & Turn Side View

153

Begin Arc:

13. Using the toes of your kicking foot, push off the floor and bring your kicking leg up at approximately a 45-degree angle. Your leg should be straight, and your kicking foot should already be in the correct position to strike your opponent.

14. As your bring your kicking leg up, your upper body should continue turning 360-degrees counterclockwise as it begins to face towards your opponent. Your back will remain straight, but not rigid.

15. Although your hands have switched position, they should still be held up (like a boxer's), with the elbows tucked in to protect the ribs and your hands up to protect your head.

16. Your head is up and facing towards your opponent, while your eyes continue to remain in contact with your opponent throughout the entire kick.

Begin Arc
Foot Position

Note: If you are like the vast majority of martial artists, you will have one leg that is very good at kicking and the other that seems to lag behind. One thing that I do to correct this, is to perform 15 repetitions on my weak leg for every 10 repetitions that I perform with my strong leg. This works well for me and is a training technique you may want to try yourself.

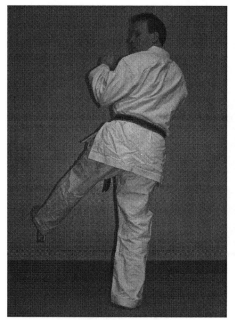

Begin Arc Front View   *Begin Arc Side View*

Peak of Arc:

17. Your base leg foot should now have moved approximately 45-degrees counterclockwise by pivoting on the ball of your foot, while the knee on your base leg remains slightly bent. Your kicking leg has now moved up to your opponent's head height, although still at a 45-degree angle to your opponentsleft.

Peak of Arc
Foot Position

18. Your kicking foot remains in the correct striking position throughout the entire sequence.
19. Your upper body, with the kicking leg side of your body remaining closer to your opponent than your base leg side, continues to move in a clockwise direction and should be facing at approximately a 45-degree angle to the left of your opponent, while continuing to lean back slightly.
20. Your head should still be up and facing towards your opponent, while your eyes continue to remain in contact with your opponent throughout the entire kick.

Note: At the end of your workout, execute a Reverse Crescent Kick as slow as you can, while maintaining strict form and control. Pay close attention to how each body part feels while executing each individual phase of the kick.

Peak of Arc Front View   *Peak of Arc Side View*

155

Impact:

21. Your base leg foot should now have moved approximately another 45-degrees counterclockwise by pivoting on the ball of your foot. At the moment of impact, your entire base leg foot should be in contact with the ground and gripping it.

Impact Foot Position

22. Your upper body, with the kicking leg side of your body remaining closer to your opponent than your base leg side, should now be facing almost directly at your opponent, while continuing to lean back slightly. At the moment of impact, your entire body should tighten to add power to the kick, as your foot continues to travel on a straight and level "Path of Trajectory" through the target.

23. Notice how your kicking foot, kicking leg, hips, back, shoulders, and head are all in alignment at the initial moment of "Impact." Also, notice how the toes of the kicking foot are pulled back towards your body and pointed up. This helps insure that contact with the target is made with the outside edge of your heel, not your ankle!

24. Your head should still be facing towards your opponent. Eye contact with your opponent is maintained at all times.

Note: A sharp exhalation of air or KIAA!, should be executed at the initial moment of impact in order to assist in tightening your body, which in turn will help add power to your kick.

Impact Front View   *Impact Side View*

Follow Through:

25. Depending on your foot position during "Impact," your base leg foot will either continue to pivot approximately 30-degrees counterclockwise, or it will remain in contact with the ground and gripping it, while in approximately the same position it was in during "Impact." In either case, the knee on your base leg will remain slightly bent.

26. Your upper body is now facing directly towards your opponent and leaning back slightly. Although your body is in this position, your back will remain straight but not rigid.

27. Your kicking leg foot should continue along exactly the same straight and level path it followed from the "Peak of Arc" to "Impact." Your foot should still remain at your opponent's head height, although it should now be at a 45-degree angle to your opponents right.

28. Your head should still be facing towards your opponent. Eye contact with your opponent is maintained at all times.

Follow Through Foot Position

Note: Although you have been confronted by an opponent, the decision to execute a technique, whether it is a kick, punch, throw, or joint technique should be determined by you and you alone, not the actions, or inactions of your opponent.

Follow Through Front View   *Follow Through Side View*

End of Arc:

29. Once again, depending on your foot position during the "Impact" phase of the kick, your base leg foot will continue to pivot anywhere from 30 to 90-degrees counterclockwise. Regardless of how far your base leg continues to pivot, the knee on your base leg will remain slightly bent.

30. Your kicking leg remains straight with the knee slightly bent. Your kicking foot is now at approximately a 45-degree angle to your left (your opponent's right), at approximately the height of your base leg knee.

31. Your upper body, with the base leg side of your body now closer to your opponent than your kicking leg side, should now be facing at approximately a 45-degree angle to the right of your opponent, although you should no longer be leaning back. Your back should be straight, but not rigid.

32. Your head should still be up with your eyes looking directly at your opponent, whether he is still standing, or lying on the ground.

End of Arc
Foot Position

Note: The principles and techniques described within this book are not specific to any particular style. The information supplied within this book is intended to be used by any martial artist, practicing any style, anywhere in the world.

End of Arc Front View　　　　*End of Arc Side View*

Return to Fighting Position:

33. Your entire body from your head to your toes, continues the 360-degree counterclockwise motion and should now be in exactly the same fighting position that you were in after switching your feet and just prior to executing this kick.

34. Your kicking leg foot also continues the 360-degree counterclockwise motion and returns to its original starting position. Your kicking leg knee will remain slightly bent as it returns to the starting position.

35. Your hands, which should have remained as close to this position as possible throughout the entire kick, are held up (like a boxer's), with the elbows tucked in to protect the ribs and your hands up to protect your head.

36. Your head should now be looking over your lead leg shoulder with your eyes in contact with your opponent.

Return to Fighting Position Foot Position

Note: Although this book details only one of the ten primary kicks and ten of its main variations. You must remember that there are nine more primary kicks, and many more variations of each of those kicks. Kicking is only one aspect of becoming a complete and effective fighter. One should also study and practice hand and elbow techniques, throwing, grappling, and joint techniques.

Return to Fighting Position Front View　　　*Return to Fighting Position Side View*

Pictorial Overview:

Fighting Position   Switch Feet   Turn

Begin Arc   Peak of Arc   Impact

FollowThrough   End of Arc   Return to Fighting Position

Training and Practice Methods

The following practice methods in this section, when performed correctly and consistently, are designed to improve your skill, speed, and power when executing a Reverse Crescent Kick. However, whether or not you improve is dependent solely upon you and your commitment to your training. When performing the exercises and drills that follow, concentrate on form and technique rather than speed or power.

Skill

The precise movement and skill you wish to obtain in the ring and on the street should be practiced correctly and consistently during training.

In other words, how you practice and train in the dojo is how you will react in the ring or on the street.

Kicking skills must be practiced correctly and consistently or speed and technique will begin to deteriorate.

Your kicking skills can be likened to an automobile. With proper maintenance and care, your automobile will last a lifetime. However, if you neglect it, your automobile will break down on you when you need it most. Since you never can tell when you will suddenly need those skills, you should strive to not only maintain them, but also to constantly improve them. Now let's take a look at some of my favorite training exercise that I use in order to improve my Reverse Crescent Kicks.

Mirror & Tape:

The mirror is without a doubt my favorite training aid. It enables me to see myself clearly and analyze my technique in minute detail. I can then correct any flaws as they become evident.

Take two pieces of colored tape (for obvious reasons), and put them on the mirror vertically (to your shoulder height) and parallel to each other approximately 4 to 5 feet apart. Roughly twice the width of your own shoulders. Now take a third piece of tape and place it horizontally across the top of the other two pieces of tape. Now you can practice your Reverse Crescent Kicks by bringing them up to the "Peak of Arc" position, and then bringing them on a straight and level line across the top of the tape and then back down to a "Fighting Position" without touching the tape (figuratively speaking), and without telegraphing the kick. This is a fantastic way to improve your Reverse Crescent Kicks and one that I strongly recommend you perform at the beginning of every workout.

Training Partner:

Training with a partner is an invaluable way to practice as a partner can tell you if you are making a mistake when executing your kick. Partners can also hold bags and pads for kicking, as well as, making the entire work out more enjoyable. A word of caution though, if your training partner spends a good deal of time talking and less time working out, then perhaps it is time to search for a new partner. Idle chatter should have no place in your training regimen. A focused workout session on your own is infinitely preferable to one spent with a poor partner.

Chair Practice:

This exercise to improve my Reverse Crescent Kick was first demonstrated to me over twenty years ago. It is still valid today and should be an important part of your training program. This exercise is very simple to perform and focuses primarily on the "Peak of Arc," "Impact," and the "Follow Through" of the kicking leg.

Start by standing in a fighting position in front of two chairs as I have demonstrated for you in the photographs below. Bring your kicking leg up at a 45-degree angle to the "Peak of Arc" position, continue along the "Path of Trajectory" by bringing your kicking leg across to the "Impact" position and continuing through to the "Follow Through" position. Then return your foot back down on the ground to its original starting position. **Remember, height isn't important, technique is!**

Starting & Finishing Position

Peak of Arc

Impact

Follow Through

162

Strength

Nearly every movement in the martial arts is carried out in opposition to a resistance. Therefore, an increase in strength means an improvement in performance.

"Stronger muscles give the athlete greater movement potential. If everything is equal, the stronger athlete will be bigger, faster, more flexible, more enduring, and less prone to injury." —Dr. Ellington Darden

"One of the benefits of strength is that it acts as a shock absorber for a muscle. Most injuries, such as tennis elbow, are caused by a force or succession of forces that cause the muscle to exceed its tensile strength. When that happens, the muscle tears. The stronger you are, the less likely that is to happen." —Michael Quinn

In order to increase muscular strength and endurance, the muscles must be worked harder than normal.

Your legs carry you everywhere you go, and are approximately 10 times stronger than your arms. Therefore the stronger your legs are, the stronger you are.

Although I have included only a few specific leg exercises in this volume, I consider the following exercises to be some of the best available for adding strength to not only your Reverse Crescent Kicks, but all of your other kicks as well. In subsequent volumes in the Achieving Kicking Excellence series, I will include several additional leg exercises which, depending on how you perform them, can develop either strength or endurance depending on the amount of weight used and repetitions performed. As with all exercises, train hard, but train smart.

Inclined Leg Press:

The Inclined Leg Press is another variation of the standard squat, which places little to no pressure on the back. Therefore, if you have back problems which preclude you from executing a standard squat, you can use this exercise as a substitute. The muscles emphasized during the leg press are the same as they are for the squat, they are the quadriceps, gluteus maximus, and the hamstrings. This exercise is used by many weightlifters when they have no spotter available, or when they can no longer safely perform free weight squats because their back or legs are too tired or sore. Remember, you should always wear shoes, weight lifting gloves and a weight lifting belt for support when you are weight lifting.

Before you begin, make sure that the weighted plates are securely fastened to the machine. Step into the machine and sit down placing your back against the padded surface, while placing your butt on the padded seat. Your legs should be straight and your feet should be approximately shoulder width apart and parallel with each other. Firmly grasp the handles located on the sides of the machine. Keeping your legs straight, reach down and release the safety bar.

From this position, slowly bend your legs, allowing your knees to move slowly towards your chest. As your knees move toward your chest, make sure that they move to the outside of your chest and not directly at the chest itself. Once your knees have reached the appropriate distance from your chest, press your legs upward and return to the starting position. Repeat this movement as often and as safely as you can. Placing your feet low on the plate or closer together, primarily emphasizes the quadriceps. However, if you place your feet farther apart, you will place more emphasis on the adductors. If you place your feet high on the plate, you will place more emphasis on the gluteals and hamstrings.

Remember:

1. **Using too heavy of a weight can cause damage to the hip and pelvic area.**
2. As with all exercises, exhale during the execution of the movement, and inhale as you return to your original starting position.
3. Do not raise your butt up, always keep your butt on the padded seat!
4. Do not lower the weight too close to your chest before pressing upward.
5. Do not bounce at the top or bottom of the movement.

Training Routine:

1. For strength use a heavier weight and perform three sets of 8 to 12 repetitions.
2. For endurance use a lighter weight and perform three to five sets of 15 to 20 repetitions per set.
3. Perform this exercise no more than 3 times per week.

Starting Position

Leg Press Position

Seated Leg Curls:

This is another excellent exercise to perform in order to isolate your hamstring muscles, which are located at the back of your thighs. This exercise, for the most part, can only be performed effectively on a seated leg curl machine. Before starting, make sure the proper amount of weight is securely attached to the machine. Begin by sitting down on the padded seat with your back firmly against the padded back of the machine. Be sure and keep your back straight at all times. **Do not hunch over or sit on the edge of the padded seat.** Place the back of your heels (Achilles Tendon area) over the lowermost padded rollers, while placing your shin (just below the front of your knees) under the uppermost set of padded rollers. Your legs should be straight at this point. Grab the sides of the bench with your hands in order to keep your upper body from moving during the course of this exercise. Utilizing your biceps femoris muscles, move your feet down and back in an arcing motion toward your hands until your feet are back as far as possible. Hold this position for a moment, and then slowly raise your legs to the starting position. Repeat this movement as often and as safely as you can.

Remember:

1. As with all exercises, exhale during the execution of the movement, and inhale as you return to your original starting position.
2. Do not raise your body up off of the padded seat during the performance of this exercise.
3. Do not do partial movements. Utilize the entire range of motion on this exercise.

Training Routine:

1. For strength use a heavier weight and perform three sets of 8 to 12 repetitions.
2. For endurance use a lighter weight and perform three to five sets of 15 to 20 repetitions per set.
3. Perform this exercise no more than 3 times per week.

Starting & Finishing Position   *Leg Curl Position*

Standing Calf Machine:

Toe raises are designed to work on the calf muscles of the lower leg, particularly the gastrocnemius and soleus muscles. This exercise also increases strength in the ankles. Before starting, make sure the proper amount of weight is securely attached to the machine. Keeping your back straight, step up onto the foot plates and place your shoulders under the shoulder pads. The balls of your feet and the toes, should be the only portions of your feet on the foot pad. Your heels and arch should be suspended in the air. Reach up with your hands and grasp the handles located to the outside of the shoulder pads. Your feet should be approximately shoulder width apart with your toes pointed forward. Slowly lower your heels. After you have lowered your heels as far as they will safely go, raise up onto the balls of your feet as high as you can. Hold this position for a moment and then slowly lower your heels back to the starting position. Repeat this movement as often and as safely as you can. You can also perform two variations of this movement by either pointing your toes inward to place more emphasis on the inner calf muscles, or outward to place more emphasis on the outer calf muscles.

Remember:

1. As with all exercises, exhale during the execution of the movement, and inhale as you return to your original starting position.
2. Keep your back straight throughout the entire movement.
3. Focus your eyes on a spot at head level in order to help keep your head up.
4. Do not bounce at the top or bottom of the movement.

Training Routine:

1. For strength use a heavier weight and perform 3 sets of 15 to 20 repetitions.
2. For endurance use a lighter weight and perform 3 to 5 sets of 25 to 30 repetitions per set.
3. Perform this exercise no more than 3 times per week.

Starting & Finishing Position

Toe Raise Position

Side-to-Side Squats with weights:

Begin by standing with your feet approximately shoulder width apart, toes pointed out at a slight angle. Lift the barbell safely and place it behind your head and across your shoulders. Your hands should maintain a wide grip on the bar for better balance. Keep your back straight and your head up throughout the entire exercise. From this position, slowly spread your feet out to approximately two to three shoulder widths apart. Slowly squat down with one leg, until you are in a side squat position. Once you have reached the side squat position, your squatting leg thigh should be parallel with the floor, while your non-squatting leg is straight out to the side. Slowly return to the starting position, and repeat this movement on the opposite side. Repeat this movement as often and as safely as you can. Always wear shoes, a weight lifting belt, and weight lifting gloves whenever you are working with free weights.

Remember:

1. Keep your back straight and rigid throughout the entire movement.
2. Focus your eyes on a spot at head level in order to help keep your head up.
3. **Use light weights only,** and do not bounce at the bottom of the squat.

Training Routine:

1. This is primarily an endurance building exercise and should be performed with a high number of repetitions (30 to 100) for several sets (3 to 10).
2. Perform this exercise no more than 3 times per week.

Starting & Finishing Position

Pre-Squat Position

Side Squat Position to the Right

Side Squat Position to the Left

Cable Machine Reverse Crescent Kicks:

This exercise places primary emphasis on the gluteus medius, gluteus minimus, and the tensor fascia latae, all of which are located on the upper outer thigh area. This exercise can be performed on a specially designed leg abduction machine, or on any cable weight machine with a floor level attachment. Before you begin, make sure that the ankle strap is securely attached to your ankle, and that the cable is securely attached to the ankle strap. It is also a good idea to have a thick sock on so that the ankle strap doesn't rub against your leg during the execution of this exercise. Start the exercise by first standing sideways to the machine with your back straight. Grasp the handle or the side of the machine for balance. **Do not grab the bars that the weights travel up and down on!** Try and keep your body as straight as possible and try not to lean over (as I have demonstrated in the photograph below), while slowly bringing your leg in front of and away from your body and to the outside of your exercising leg as far as possible. Hold this position for a moment. Then slowly bring your leg back to the starting position. Repeat this movement as often and as safely as you can. When finished with one leg, repeat the same procedure with the other leg.

Remember:

1. Perform this exercise slowly in order to obtain the maximum benefit.
2. Do not do partial movements. Utilize the entire range of motion on this exercise.

Training Routine:

1. Use light weights to start with and perform three to five sets of 25 to 30 repetitions per set.
2. Perform this exercise no more than 3 times per week.

Starting & Finishing Position   *Leg Abduction Across the Body*

168

Side-to-Side Squats:

This exercise, along with the variation using weights described on page 165, is perhaps the best overall leg exercise that you can do in order to improve the strength in your legs for kicking. Begin by standing with your feet approximately two to three shoulder widths apart, toes pointed out at a slight angle. Your hands can be either behind your head, or resting on your hips. Keep your back straight and your head up throughout the entire exercise. From this position, slowly squat down with one leg, allowing your knee to move outward in the same direction as your toes. At the same time contract your back muscles in order keep your body rigid as your perform this exercise. Slowly squat down until you are in a full side squat position with your squatting leg thigh parallel to the ground, and your non-squatting leg straight out to the side. Once you have reached the side squat position, slowly return to the starting position, and repeat this movement on the opposite side. Repeat this movement as often and as you safely can.

Remember:
1. Keep your back straight throughout the entire movement.
2. Focus your eyes on a spot at head level in order to help keep your head up.
3. Do not bounce at the bottom of the squat.
4. Do not squat lower than your thigh parallel with the floor.

Training Routine:
1. This is primarily an endurance building exercise and should be performed with a high number of repetitions (30 to 100) for several sets (3 to 10).
2. Perform this exercise no more than 3 times per week.

Starting & Finishing Position

Side Squat Position to the Right Side

Side Squat Position to the Left Side

Plyometric Ankle Bounces:

Plyometric ankle bounces are without a doubt one of the best exercises to perform in order to add explosive power to your kicks. This exercise emphasizes all of the muscles of the leg to a certain degree, from the muscles of the foot all the way up to the gluteus maximus and lower back. When performing this or any other plyometric type exercise, you should exercise extreme caution due to the amount of stress that is placed on your body from these exercises. I would advise you to perform these exercises no more than two times per week, and to give yourself at least two days rest in between each plyometric training routine. Before you begin, make sure that the area around you is clear of any obstacles.

This exercise can be performed with or without shoes. Make sure that you are wearing gi bottoms or other loose fitting pants. Begin by standing with your feet approximately shoulders width apart and your toes pointing forward. Keeping your back straight and your head up, bring your arms up into a fighting position with your hands at shoulder level. From this position, explosively bring one of your knees up as high as you can to your upper chest. As soon as your knee reaches your chest, explosively force your leg back down to the ground, but don't slam your foot into the ground. Set it down gently, but quickly. As soon as your foot touches the ground, immediately and explosively repeat the same movement with your opposite leg. Repeat this movement as often and as safely as you can alternating your legs each time.

Remember:
1. Make sure that the area around you is free of any obstacles.
2. Focus your eyes on a spot at head level in order to help keep your head up.
3. Do not slam your foot into the ground. Set it down quickly, but gently.
4. Your back should be kept as straight as possible at all times.
5. Do not perform plyometric type exercises more than twice per week.

Training Routine:
1. Perform one set of 10 to 20 repetitions per leg, no more than 2 times per week.
2. Work up to two sets of 20 to 50 repetitions per leg, no more than 2 times per week.

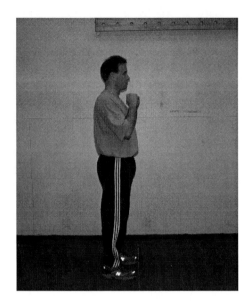

Starting & Finishing Position

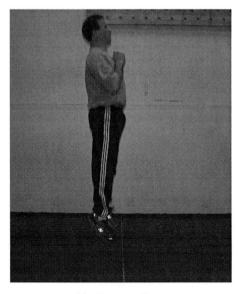

Ankle Bounce Position

Lunges without weights:

This exercise, along with the variation using weights described on page 213, is perhaps one of the best overall leg exercises that you can do in order to improve both strength and flexibility in your legs for kicking, especially when executing an Axe Kick. Begin by standing with your feet approximately shoulder width apart and your toes pointed forward. Your hands can be either behind your head, or resting on your hips. Keep your back straight and your head up throughout the entire exercise. From this position, slowly step forward approximately two and a half to three shoulder widths. Once you have reached the forward lunge position, your forward leg thigh should be parallel with the floor, while your rear leg is straight. The entire bottom surface of both feet should be flat on the ground. Hold this position for a moment, then slowly return to the starting position. Once you return to the starting position, repeat this movement on the opposite side. Repeat this movement as often and as safely as you can.

Remember:
1. Keep your back straight throughout the entire movement.
2. Focus your eyes on a spot at head level in order to help keep your head up.
3. Do not bounce at the bottom of the forward lunge.
4. Do not squat lower than your front thigh parallel with the floor.

Training Routine:
1. This is primarily an endurance building exercise and should be performed with a high number of repetitions (30 to 100) for several sets (3 to 10).
2. Perform this exercise no more than 3 times per week.

Starting & Finishing Position

Lunge Position with the Left Leg Forward

Lunge Position with the Right Leg Forward

Speed

The speed of your kicks during training should be at the same speed you plan to use during self-defense or during competition.

As I stated earlier in this section, how you practice and train in the dojo is how you will react in the ring or on the street.

The primary component of speed under pressure is not physical, but mental. Therefore, you must stay focused and concentrate.

Your mind controls your body. Therefore, you must keep control of your mind in order to perform at your optimum level.

If you think that you're slow, you will be slow. If however you believe that you can be faster, you will be faster.

Now let's take a look at some of my favorite speed training exercises that I use to increase the speed in my Reverse Crescent Kicks.

Ankle Weights:

This is my favorite piece of exercise equipment that I use in order to improve the speed of not only my Reverse Crescent Kicks, but all other kicks as well. Properly used ankle weights can improve your speed and hitting power in your legs as well as increasing muscular stamina. Improperly used however, they can cause a variety of injuries to the joints and connective tissues. This is not only detrimental to your body, but it also causes you to lose valuable training time. When practicing your kicks with ankle weights, you should make sure that they are securely fastened around your ankles and not loose. Start with 2 lbs. on each ankle and gradually build up the weight over time. Don't rush it. Perform your kicks no faster than 3/4 speed. Concentrate on technique and form. Remember that your legs will weaken faster utilizing the ankle weights. Therefore, caution must be exercised so that you do not injure your knees or hips. Any kicking drill or exercise can be utilized with the ankle weights, with the notable exceptions of plyometric exercises and reactionary drills. I do not recommend using any kind of weight when performing plyometric exercises. These exercises are of such high intensity that no additional weight is needed. Reactionary drills require you to kick as fast as you can in response to an outside stimulus. Therefore ankle weights would be a hindrance rather than a benefit.

Quick Draw:

This is an excellent reactionary drill and requires the use of a training partner. I got the idea of this training method from watching western movies when I was a kid. Picture the following scene from any western movie.

The sheriff looks out the window of the saloon onto the dust-covered Main Street of town where the outlaw who killed his father stands waiting. A tied down six-gun slung low on his right thigh. The sheriff steps through the saloon doors and out onto the porch, his eyes never leaving the outlaw. He walks off the porch and out onto the street where he turns toward the outlaw. They stand facing each other from no more than 50 feet. Neither one moves. Suddenly the outlaw makes a move for his gun. BANG! The outlaw falls backward, dead, a .45 caliber bullet lodged in his brain. The sheriff holsters his Colt Peacemaker and walks back into the saloon.

Now you may be asking yourself how is this going to help your kicking skills. The answer is really quite simple. I have modified the classic western shoot out, or quick draw, by utilizing a training partner and your kicks instead of a Colt Peacemaker. Begin by having your training partner stand in front of you out of kicking range. You will be facing him in a fighting position. At your partner's discretion, he will make a prearranged movement, which will be the indicator for you to execute a kick as quickly as you can toward your partner. That indicator can be anything from a snapping of the fingers to the blinking of an eye. Use your imagination. Kicks can be performed one at a time, two or three at a time, using the same leg or alternating legs. Be creative and design your own unique routine. This exercise can also be utilized with a force bag or kicking paddle. However, extreme care must be utilized so that you do not accidentally miss your target and end up hitting your training partner. That doesn't seem to go over to well with training partners.

Water Training:

This particular training method requires a rather large piece of training equipment, a full-sized swimming pool. The deep end of the pool needs to be at least 6 feet deep in order for you to practice your kicks in mid-chest to shoulder deep water. This method of practicing your kicking technique is identical to performing the primary kick and all of its variations in the air. However, always keep in mind that when you are practicing in water, you will always be kicking against a constant state of resistance.

Start off by practicing your kicking technique at 1/4 speed until your kicking skills become easier and more natural. As you become progressively more efficient in your kicking skills, you will gradually increase your speed until you are performing your kicks at full speed. Remember, that if you do your Reverse Crescent Kicks at your actual head height, as you approach the "Peak of Arc" position, your kicking foot will exit the water and will not reenter the water until shortly after the "Follow Through" phase of the kick. Therefore, I recommend that you keep your kicking foot totally submerged in the water throughout the entire execution of the kick. Although your kicking foot will not be at head height, keeping it submerged will force you to kick against a constant state of resistance the entire time. Even though you are practicing in the water, never sacrifice proper technique for speed or power.

It is imperative that you take all necessary precautions when practicing this technique. If at all possible, utilize this training method only with a training partner in case of any unforeseen accidents.

Jump Rope:

Jumping rope is not only a time-honored method for building endurance in the sport of boxing, but it is also an excellent method of building rhythmic foot movement and speed for all sports that require foot and hand coordination.

Proper Repetitive Practice:

Regardless of the activity, the more you practice the faster you will become, provided proper technique is maintained throughout the exercise. Notice the difference in the speed of your kick from the very first time you practice it, to the 1,000th time, the 5,000th time, the 10,000th time, etc. Which one was faster?

176

Power

Force = Mass x Acceleration

In other words, the faster you are, multiplied by the greatest amount of muscular mass that you can generate behind your kick, equals striking power. Now let's take a look at my two favorite pieces of training equipment that I utilize in order to improve my kicking power when executing a Reverse Crescent Kick. They are the force bag (hand held kicking shield) and the kicking paddle.

Force Bag:

The force bag or kicking shield is a hand held pad or bag, that is usually made out of vinyl or leather with a foam filled core. There are usually two sets of handles located on the bag, two on the back portion of the bag, and one on each side of the bag. If utilized correctly, these bags are invaluable as training aids in order to increase the speed and power in your Reverse Crescent Kicks.

Begin by having your bag holder grasp the handles located on the sides of the bag. He should hold the bag straight out in front of him (one arm above the other), and perpendicular to the ground, with the bottom of the force bag at shoulder height. He should position himself in a parallel stance with his legs about one and a half to two shoulder widths apart. As the kicker, you want to aim your kicks about 4 inches in from the closest edge of the bag, and at the level of the vulnerable points you are striking at. At all times you must be extremely careful when kicking so that you do not accidentally kick your training partner. They tend to get a little grouchy when kicked.

As the bag holder, you do not want to get in the habit of being just a bag holder. Utilize this time to improve your defensive skills by relaxing your body the entire time until just before the moment of impact. Make sure that the bottom edge of the bag is perpendicular to the ground and facing directly at the kicker. It should not be at an angle. You can utilize any kicking routine you can think of with the force bag. You can practice single kicks, multiple kicks (one leg at a time or alternating legs), the Quick Draw method, etc. You are only limited by your own imagination.

Kicking Paddle:

The kicking paddle is a very versatile piece of training equipment that, when utilized correctly, can help improve not only the power in your Reverse Crescent Kick, but also your accuracy, speed, timing, and footwork. Another benefit of training with the kicking paddle is to help you to improve your ability to obtain and maintain the correct kicking distance between you and your opponent. Because it offers so much versatility in your training routine, the kicking paddle can also be used to simulate the offensive and defensive movements of an actual opponent.

You can utilize full force Reverse Crescent Kicks on the kicking paddles without worrying about damaging them. However, when using the kicking paddle or any other piece of training equipment, you must exercise caution so that you don't inadvertently hurt yourself by hyper-extending your knee, twisting an ankle, etc., or hurting your training partner by inadvertently hitting him or her. This is why the kicking paddle consists of the handle and the separate target area. Strike the target area when kicking, not the hands of your training partner. There are numerous routines, which you can utilize when working with the kicking paddle. Some of the routines I utilize in order to improve my Reverse Crescent Kicks are exactly the same as those used when kicking the force bag. While other routines are designed to simulate actual sparring conditions.

Running:

Running is a must for anyone who is serious about self-defense or competition. I will not go into any details about running itself other than to say that it should be an essential part of any martial artists training. There are several good books on running available, and any one of them would be an invaluable addition to your library.

Running Stairs:

In addition to regular running, running stairs is an excellent method of building the muscles in the legs while at the same time building up your aerobic capacity and endurance. However, extreme caution must be exercised at all times to avoid injuring yourself while performing this or any exercise described in this book.

Relaxation and Tension:

Muscle contractions used during training should duplicate those used in self-defense or competition.

If you do not utilize the proper tension and relaxation principles in the dojo when kicking, you will not use them correctly on the street or in the ring. This principle is very simple yet seems to be very difficult for individuals to follow. Physiologically speaking a relaxed muscle is able to react faster than a tense muscle. Therefore, you want to remain as relaxed as possible from the time you initiate your kick until just before the moment of impact. At this point your entire body should tighten up to add power to your kick. Immediately after the moment of impact, your muscles should once again relax in order to facilitate a faster "Follow Through" after impact with your target. I have found that the best method for practicing this technique is to perform the Water Training method, which I described earlier in this section. Perform this technique slowly and concentrate on proper technique while remaining totally relaxed throughout the kicking process until just before the moment of impact. At this point tighten all of the muscles in your body and hold them that way for just an instant. **Remember,** once impact has been made, relax immediately and complete your kick.

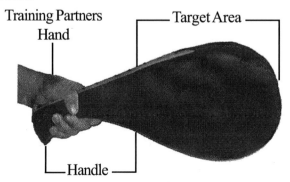

Training Partners Hand — Target Area —

Handle

Kicking Paddle

Trouble Shooting Guide

In this chapter, I will present some of the most common questions concerning mistakes that I have encountered from students when attempting to perform the Back Leg Reverse Crescent Kick or any one of its many variations. I will then attempt to provide a generalized answer to each of those questions. Although one must keep in mind that there is no way to provide the appropriate answer to each person without actually seeing him or her perform the kick in person. When you have a problem, always refer back to the instruction section that covers that particular movement in which you are having a problem. One of my instructors once imparted upon me a small piece of wisdom that I would now like to share with you concerning mistakes. "If you suddenly find yourself making mistakes, go back to the beginning." In other words, you can never practice or study the basic techniques enough, for they are the foundation in which all other techniques are based.

Why do I always seem to be hitting with the wrong part of my foot?

This is usually caused by one of three things. (1) You are not bringing your toes back and towards your shin exposing the outside edge of your heel as the striking implement. This happens quite often when one tries to "reach" for the target, rather than having already created the proper striking distance. (2) You are not bringing the kicking knee up along the correct "Path of Trajectory" before executing the kick. This tends to make the kicking leg "swoop" when executed rather than following the correct line of trajectory towards the target. When your kicking leg "swoops", the toes on your kicking foot are usually what strikes the target instead of the outside edge of the heel. (3) You are too close to your opponent and the outside of your ankle or shin is what makes contact with the target area on your opponent. Rather than the correct striking implement, which in this case is the outside edge of your heel. **Always create the proper striking distance before you kick!**

Why do I always seem to be hitting my opponent's shoulders every time I kick?

This particular problem is almost exclusively caused by one thing. You are attempting to kick from the ground in a "swooping" motion rather than bringing the kicking leg and foot along the correct "Path of Trajectory." One other possibility is that you may need to spend a little more time on improving your flexibility.

Every time I try and use a Reverse Crescent Kick with a training partner, they always seem to see it coming and move out of the way!

This particular problem can be related not only to improper technique, but also to inappropriate use of the Reverse Crescent Kick. Let's look at technique first. (1) You may not be following the correct "Path of Trajectory" prior to execution of the technique, or you may be making some unconscious body movement prior to executing the kick, and therefore are telegraphing your intentions to you opponent. (2) Another possible problem is that you may not yet have the entire sequence of movements flowing together to where they all are one continuous motion. You may be pausing during the execution of the kick and not be aware of it. The best way to correct both of these problems is to practice in front of a mirror. (3) The other possibility is that your technique is fine, but your application of the kick is incorrect. Are you attempting to use the Reverse Crescent Kick as a finishing technique? Or as a "set-up" technique? Remember that for the most part, the Reverse Crescent Kick is a "set-up" technique rather than a finishing technique, although it can effectively be used in both instances. Try limiting your use of the kick when sparring and always try and set up the Reverse Crescent Kick by utilizing another technique before executing it. Whether it is another kick, punch or even simply footwork.

Every time I hit my opponent, my Reverse Crescent Kicks aren't very effective!

There are several possible reasons for this. (1) You may not be striking the correct vital or vulnerable point. (2) You may be utilizing the incorrect striking implement. (3) You may be hitting your opponent with a "surface strike," rather than "striking through" your opponent. (4) You may not be utilizing the correct relaxation and tension principles during the execution of the kick. Or, (5) it may be a combination of any of the above mentioned reasons.

Why do my Reverse Crescent Kicks miss the target more times that they hit it?

The most common solution to this problem is that you have to make sure that you are looking at your opponent during the entire time you are executing the kick. Stay focused! Another possible solution is that you need to practice the "Peak of Arc" through "Impact" and continuing to the "Follow Through" position, portion of the kick more often and slower until your accuracy improves.

It seems like every time I hit a solid target, my kicking foot just stops!

This can most often be attributed to a person utilizing a "surface strike" on his opponent with the kick rather than "striking through" his opponent. In order to correct this you need to work on two primary areas. (1) Executing the "Follow Through" phase of the kick faster with the kicking leg after "Impact," and (2) Practicing the relaxation and tension movements before, during, and after impact.

I can do a Back Leg Reverse Crescent Kick fairly well, but when it comes to some of the other Reverse Crescent Kicks, I always seem to have problems!

The important thing to remember here is that all of the Reverse Crescent Kick variations are based on the primary kick, Back Leg Reverse Crescent Kick. If you are executing the Back Leg Reverse Crescent Kick correctly, then you need to focus more of your attention on not only the additional moves associated with each particular variation, but also in the ability to flow in one continuous motion from the additional portion of the particular Reverse Crescent Kick variation, to the Back Leg

Reverse Crescent Kick itself.

Why do I lose my balance every time I kick?

There are several possible reasons for this. (1) You may not be keeping your head up and looking at your opponent while executing the kick. (2) You may be attempting to imitate a bird by waving your arms all over the place instead of having them in control and next to your body. (3) Your center of gravity may not be over your base leg. (4) Over-extending or "reaching" with the kicking leg. (5) Leaning to far backward, or even forward with your upper body during the execution of the kick. (6) Balancing on the ball of your foot rather than the entire base foot when kicking.

How come I just can't seem to get any power into my Reverse Crescent Kick?

Power in a Reverse Crescent Kick is generated by the correct execution of all phases of the kick. The most important being proper technique. For arguments sake, let us assume (and you know what happens when you make an assumption) that you are performing all of the "movement" phases of the kick correctly. I would then have to say that you are probably not performing the tension and relaxation portion of the kick correctly, as this is the most difficult aspect of the kick to perform correctly. Remember that the entire body should be in a relaxed state throughout the entire execution of the kick, except immediately before impact. When the entire body should turn into a solid, rigid mass to support and add power to the kick, and then immediately relax again to add speed to the "Follow Through."

Why is my Reverse Crescent Kick so slow?

Anything is slow the first few hundred or even a thousand times you do them. Speed is not important to learning, be patient and practice until the kick becomes instinctive in nature. After you become comfortable with the execution of the kick, then you can gradually add more speed when executing it. If you are still experiencing a slow kick, you may be too tense when executing the kick and this will greatly decrease your speed. Another potential problem could be that you "see" yourself as being slow. If you want to be fast, think fast!

Why is my Reverse Crescent Kick not hitting my opponent in the "Impact" position during the straight and level phase of the "Path of Trajectory?"

The primary cause for this is improper pivoting on the ball of the base leg foot during the execution of the kick. What is the foot position of your base leg foot during the "Impact" phase of the kick? Are your toes pointed toward your opponent? Is your heel pointed toward your opponent? How about the outside edge of your foot, is that pointed toward your opponent? Or, is the inside edge of your foot pointed toward your opponent?

Remember that often times we are unable to see clearly are own mistakes. That is why a qualified and competent instructor, and a good training partner is so vitally important to your martial arts training.

Reverse Crescent Kick Applications

In this chapter, I will discuss some of the basic applications for the Back Leg Reverse Crescent Kick and the ten variations discussed in this book. Please keep in mind that the numerous applications of each kick could fill an entire book. Therefore, I will limit this section to one application per kick. A second series of books detailing the combat and tournament applications of each kick is in the works and will be published following the release of this ten volume series. Keep in mind that the photographs in this section are staged in order to give you the best possible view of each technique in order to help you learn from them. The actual execution of any of these kicks should be instantaneously (without thought), and in one continuous motion. My assistant and I have intentionally made some errors that can be seen in some of these photographs in order to help you correct some common mistakes. See if you can spot them before I tell you them at the end of each kicking application.

For reference purposes, Ron Dunlap will be the attacker while I will be the defender in this series of photographs. Ron is wearing a black uniform, while I am wearing a white uniform.

Back Leg Reverse Crescent Kick:

1. You and your opponent are facing each other in what is commonly referred to as a Closed Position, meaning that each of you has the same leg forward and the front of your bodies facing in different directions. In this photograph, both Ron and I have our left legs forward, while the front of Ron's body is basically facing away from the camera, while the front of my body is facing toward the camera.

2. By reading your opponents body language, you discern that he is going to initiate an attack by attempting to punch you with his right hand. Immediately, upon sensing this, you begin to initiate your kick.

3. Always make sure to follow the correct upward "Path of Trajectory" arcing motion up to the "Peak of Arc," which should be at the exact height of your intended target, before beginning the straight and level "Path of Trajectory." Remember to protect yourself at all times and not to telegraph your intentions to your attacker.

4. Execute the kick. Ideally you want to strike your opponent when he is midway through his committed technique. By the time your opponents eyes have registered the fact that you have moved your leg, his brain should be registering the pain as your kick connects to the vital or vulnerable point you have just initially struck. Don't forget to "Follow Through" with your kicking leg after impact.

Did you notice anything wrong or improper in this series of photographs? Take another look. See them now?

If you look closely at photograph number four; you can see that although I struck through my target correctly, I left my kicking foot "hanging" in the air. As you can clearly see in the photograph, both of Ron's hands are up and very close to my kicking leg. It would be very easy for Ron to grab my kicking leg from this position and put me in a world of hurt. Always make sure that your kick is just as fast, if not faster, traveling from "Impact" back to a "Fighting Position," as it is traveling from your initial "Fighting Position" to "Impact."

Although this may seem like a very minor detail, it is very important to the overall effectiveness of your kick. No matter how you add it up, ninety-nine pennies does not add up to one dollar. All aspects of a properly executed kick are much like pennies in a dollar. Every one of the one hundred pennies must be present in order to have a complete dollar, just like every aspect of a kick must be performed correctly in order to have a proper kick.

Step-Back Turning Reverse Crescent Kick:

1. You and your attacker are facing each other in what is commonly referred to as an Open Position, meaning that one of you, in this case Ron, has his left leg forward while I have my right leg forward. This will result in both of our bodies facing in the same direction. In this case, both Ron and I have our backs facing toward the camera.

2. Your opponent initiates and attack by attempting to punch you with his left hand. As soon as you sense your opponents attack, you "step-back" in order to avoid the attack and in preparation for executing your kick.

3. As soon as your foot starts to set down after stepping back, you immediately begin to initiate your kick. Remember to protect yourself at all times and not to telegraph your intentions to your opponent. As you can see in this photograph, you are in a very dangerous position.

4. Execute the kick. Be sure to correctly execute not only the upward "Path of Trajectory" up to the "Peak of Arc" position and the downward "Path of Trajectory" from the "Follow Through" position back to a "Fighting Position," but also the straight and level portion of the kick from the "Peak of Arc" to the "Follow Through" position.

Did you notice anything wrong or improper in this series of photographs? Take another look. See them now?

If you look closely at photograph number four; you will see that I have struck Ron not with the outside edge of my heel, but with the outside edge of my ankle. Not exactly the preferred striking implement with any kick, let alone the Reverse Crescent Kick. **Always** strike the correct vital or vulnerable point on your opponent with the correct striking implement. This not only maximizes the effectiveness of your kick, but it also minimizes the possibility of injury to you.

Switch Turning Reverse Crescent Kick:

1. Once again, you and your opponent are facing each other in what is commonly referred to as an Open Position.

2. Sensing my opponents impending attack, and wishing to confuse him while repositioning my body, I switch the position of my feet utilizing a scissors type motion. This results in my opponent and I now being in a Closed Position.

3. As soon as I switch my feet, I want to begin to initiate my kick. Remember to maintain eye contact with your opponent. If you look closely at this photograph, you can see that having my back facing towards my opponent leaves me in a very dangerous position. Always use extreme caution when turning your back towards your opponent.

4. One of the many reasons why you want to make a correct "arcing" motion with your leg during the upward "Path of Trajectory," is to avoid the possibility of your opponent grabbing your kicking leg, or inadvertently hitting your opponent's shoulders, rather than his head.

Did you notice anything wrong or improper in this series of photographs? Take another look. See them now?

If you look closely at photograph number four; you can clearly see that although I have struck Ron with a Reverse Crescent Kick, I did not strike him correctly with the outside edge of my heel, instead I struck Ron with the outside edge of my ankle. This is not only incorrect, but it also greatly lessens the impact potential of your kick. Along with using the incorrect striking implement, I failed to strike the correct vital or vulnerable point on Ron's head. Instead, I struck the ear area of Ron's head, rather than the jaw or temple. Combined with using the incorrect striking implement, not striking the correct vital or vulnerable point even further lessens the impact potential of your kick.

To give you an example, correctly executing all aspects of a Reverse Crescent Kick is like explosively and suddenly backhanding a tennis ball back across the net with a tennis racket. However, not doing so can be likened to trying the same thing with a feather, rather than the tennis racket. You figure out which one you want to use on an opponent, the tennis racket or the feather.

Off-Setting Turning Reverse Crescent Kick:

1. You and your opponent are facing each other in a Closed Position. However, in this case, the front of Ron's body is basically in a squared off position and facing toward me, while my back is facing toward the camera.

2. Your opponent attempts to lunge forward and punch you with his right hand. As soon as you sense your opponent's impending attack, you begin to offset his attack by moving your right foot to the right and at a 45-degree angle to your opponent. Which you immediately follow with...

3. ...moving your left leg to the right to complete the "off-setting" movement. This will effectively move your body out of the line of attack, and puts you in a very advantageous position to initiate a counterattack against your attacker. Remember to keep your hands up and protect yourself at all times.

4. As your left foot completes the "off-setting" movement, you should already begin to execute your kick. Since you are kicking in the direction of your opponents outstretched arm, you must make sure that you are executing your upward "Path of Trajectory" correctly, or you will hit your opponent's arm instead of his head.

5. Begin to initiate the kick. Ideally, you will want to strike your attacker while he is off balance and in a vulnerable position. As seen in this picture. Not only has Ron left his right arm fully extended, but he has also dropped his left hand. In addition to that, his center of gravity and balance is now in front of his feet rather than over them. Bad for Ron, but great for me!

6. Execute the kick.

Did you notice anything wrong or improper in this series of photographs? Take another look. See them now?

If you look closely at photographs number four, five, and six; you can see that by making the choice to execute a Turning Reverse Crescent Kick, I am bringing my kick up in front of my opponent not only where he can clearly see it, but also where he already has his arm outstretched and could attempt to block or grab my kicking leg. In this particular instance, a better choice would have been to execute a Turning Back Kick where my kicking leg would have traveled beneath Ron's outstretched arm where it would have not only been harder for him to see (if at all), but it would also be farther away from his outstretched arm. Which he could have used to grab my kicking leg as it traveled along its upward "Path of Trajectory."

This is one of the reasons why it is so important to learn not only **"How"** to kick correctly, but also the **"Who, What, Where, When, and Why"** of kicking. These principles, although discussed briefly in Chapter Three, will be discussed in great detail in an upcoming ten volume series which will focus on the combat and tournament applications of each of the ten primary kicks and their respective variations.

It is so vitally important to not only know **"How"** to execute all of the primary kicks and their variations, but also **"When"** to use them. If you have to screw two boards together, use a screwdriver. If a board is too long, use a saw. If you have to nail two boards together, use a hammer. Use the appropriate tool for each situation.

Front Leg Reverse Crescent Kick:

1. You and your opponent are facing each other in an Open Position. Your opponent attempts to punch you with his left hand. As you can see in this photograph, any attempt to execute a Reverse Crescent Kick from this position would be ineffective, as I am too far away to strike Ron in the head. However, ...

2. ... I am in an effective kicking range to strike Ron's fully extended arm that he has so graciously presented to me for a target. Therefore, I begin to initiate my kick.

3. Execute the kick. Remember that you never want to sacrifice technique for speed.

Did you notice anything wrong or improper in this series of photographs? Take another look. See them now?

If you look closely at photograph number one; you can see that Ron and I are not at an effective punching range, and that I don't have to do anything at all to avoid Ron's attack. You can also clearly see that Ron has left his arm hanging out in the air after trying to punch me rather than retracting it to the correct on-guard or boxing position. This is bad for Ron, but a great opportunity for me. Know what a mistake is, and when your opponent makes one, take advantage of it.

Turning Reverse Crescent Kick:

1. You and your opponent are facing each other in a Closed Position. While currently at an effective kicking range, you are just at the outer limit for an effective punching range.

2. Therefore, your opponent leans forward in an attempt to "close the distance" with you and initiates a punch to your head with his left hand. In an attempt to deceive your opponent, you begin to lean back in order to avoid his attack.

3. As you lean back, you suddenly turn and begin to initiate your kick. Always maintain eye contact with your opponent and keep your hands up in order to protect your head and upper body.

4. Execute the kick. Even though a lot of these photographs only show the "Impact" phase of the kick, remember to always "Follow Through" and get your kicking foot back down on the ground as fast as possible.

Did you notice anything wrong or improper in this series of photographs? Take another look. See them now?

Take a look at photograph number three, even though I am still looking at my opponent, see how I have left my back open and exposed to my attacker by not executing both my footwork and turn quick enough. This is not only incorrect, but it is also a very dangerous thing to do. Any technique that you do should be executed so fast that you don't even realize that you have executed it until after it has been completed. **Never turn your back on your opponent.**

Note: **If you look closely at the photograph of the pocketwatch above, you will see a cutout view of the face of the watch, which exposes a number of gears in various sizes and positions that you normally would not see. These gears are representative of all of the various aspects of a Reverse Crescent Kick, which like each individual component of a Reverse Crescent Kick, are of a very high quality and that, like a finely crafted pocketwatch, are skillfully combined with one another to create an exquisitely efficient product.**

191

Spinning Reverse Crescent Kick:

1. You and your opponent are facing each other in an Open Position. However, at the current time, you are too far away from your opponent to effectively execute a kick.

2. Therefore, you step forward in order to close the distance, which will enable you the opportunity to execute your kick. As the ball of your base leg foot touches the ground after you have stepped forward, you...

3. ...turn and begin to initiate the kick. Remember, to always keep your eyes on your opponent and your hands up in order to protect your head and upper body.

4. Execute the kick. Notice how extremely vulnerable you are in this position. This is why you have got to be so precise in not only the physical aspects or **"How"** to execute the kick correctly, but also the circumstantial aspects or the **"Who, What, Where, When and Why"** for attempting to execute the kick.

Did you notice anything wrong or improper in this series of photographs? Take another look. See them now?

If you look closely at photograph number three, you can see that I have intentionally left my back facing towards Ron in an attempt to draw him in towards me. This is a very tricky technique to execute correctly, and one that I don't recommend unless you have had thousands of hours of quality practice.

Now if you look closely at photograph number four, you can see that Ron has fallen for my deception and has moved forward slightly, which enabled me to effectively strike Ron with my kick. This can be a very effective strategic technique if utilized appropriately in the correct situation.

Hopping/Sliding Forward Reverse Crescent Kick:

1. You and your opponent are facing each other in a Closed Position. However, at the moment your opponent is just out of kicking range.

2. Therefore, in order to close the distance with your opponent, you execute a hop/slide forward. As you are moving forward you should begin initiating the kick so that it strikes your opponent just after you reach the end of your hop or slide forward.

3. Begin to execute the kick, while adhering to all of the correct principles involved in order to attain the maximum amount of efficiency and effectiveness with your kick.

4. As you hop or slide forward, while bringing your kicking leg up to the "Peak of Arc" position, you can cover anywhere from a few inches to two feet with a correctly executed hop or slide. The exact distance will vary from application to application, but one factor remains. You must be exact in judging the correct distance, or your kick will not attain its maximum effectiveness.

Did you notice anything wrong or improper in this series of photographs? Take another look. See them now?

If you look at photograph number two, you can see that I clearly executed the hop or slide forward independent of the actual kick. Although this should initially be done in practice until you can effectively combine the two, it should not be done in an actual self-defense situation. If you can not execute a technique perfectly in practice without thinking, you shouldn't try it on the street or in the ring.

Cross-Over Reverse Crescent Kick:

1. You and your opponent are facing each other in an Open Position. While currently at the outer edges of an effective kicking range, you need to "close the distance" with your opponent in order to effectively utilize your kick.

2. Therefore, in order to close the distance with your opponent, you execute a "cross-over" motion moving forward. As you are moving forward, you should begin initiating the kick so that it strikes your opponent just after you reach the end of your "cross-over" motion.

3. Begin to initiate the kick, while adhering to all of the correct principles involved in order to attain the maximum amount of efficiency and effectiveness with your kick.

4. Execute the kick. As you "cross-over," bringing your kicking leg up to the "Peak of Arc" position, you can cover anywhere from a few inches to ;your shoulder width. The exact distance will vary from application to application, but one factor remains. You must be exact in judging the correct distance or your kick will not attain its maximum effectiveness.

195

Did you notice anything wrong or improper in this series of photographs? Take another look. See them now?

In photograph number two, you can clearly see that I have paused for a moment midway through executing the "cross-over" phase of this kick, resulting in my legs being momentarily crossed. This is a very unstable and potentially dangerous position to be in. As soon as the ball of your rear foot touches the ground after "crossing-over" your lead leg, you should have already begun initiating your kick. This is not a mere walking type motion, this is a "faster than you can blink" sprinting type motion. Now if you look closely at photograph number four, you can see that I am balancing on the ball of my base leg foot at the moment of "Impact," instead of having it flat on the ground like it should be.

This is an **<u>extremely bad habit</u>** to get into, and one that needs to be corrected immediately. Always adhere to the correct execution of movement during all phases of executing any kick, punch, or strike.

Hopping/Sliding Backward Reverse Crescent Kick:

1. You and your opponent are facing each other in a Closed Position. While currently at an effective punching and even grappling range, you are too close to effectively utilize your kicks.

2. Therefore, in order to create a more effective kicking range and in an attempt to deceive your opponent, you begin to execute a hop or slide backwards while pushing off of your opponent. Even though you are in effect moving away from your opponent, always maintain eye contact with your opponent and keep your hands up in order to protect your head and upper body.

3. As soon as you hop or slide backward, begin to initiate your kick. This hop or slide backward should have taken you out of an effective punching and/or grappling range, and put you into an effective kicking range.

4. Immediately after hopping or sliding backward, bring your kicking leg up along the correct upward "Path of Trajectory" and execute your kick. You can cover anywhere from a few inches to two feet with a correctly executed hop or slide backward. However, you must be exact in judging the correct distance, or your kick will not attain its maximum effectiveness.

Did you notice anything wrong or improper in this series of photographs? Take another look. See them now?

If you look closely at photographs number two, three and four, you can clearly see another example of using the appropriate tool for each particular situation. In this case, I believe that there were many different options that I could have used that would have been more effective than a Reverse Crescent Kick. Study and learn, then adapt and improvise.

Jump Turning Reverse Crescent Kick:

1. You and your opponent are facing each other in a Closed Position.

2. Sensing my opponents impending attack, and wishing to confuse him while increasing the power in my kick, I jump up in the air and start turning.

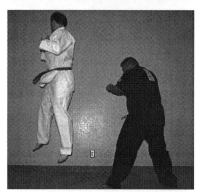

3. As soon as I jump up into the air and begin turning, I begin to initiate my kick. Because of the very unstable and potentially dangerous position you are in when jumping, you want to make this movement so quick that you don't even realize that you have done it until after your feet are back down on the ground.

198

4. Always make sure to follow the complete and correct "Path of Trajectory" arcing motion throughout the entire kick. Your "Peak of Arc" should be at the exact height of your intended target. Regardless of whether you are jumping, standing, or lying on the ground when you kick. Remember to protect yourself at all times and not to telegraph your intentions to your attacker.

Did you notice anything wrong or improper in this series of photographs? Take another look. See them now?

If you look closely at photograph number four, you can see that I have committed perhaps one of the biggest mistakes made when executing this type of aerial kick, kicking over my opponent's head rather than correctly kicking the selected vulnerable or vital point within a specific target area. When executed correctly, and at the proper time, aerial kicking can be a very effective technique to have in your kicking arsenal.

Remember that, even though you may be proficient in kicking while one foot remains on the ground, that does not mean that you will automatically transfer that skill over to the execution of aerial kicks. Aerial kicking is an art form unto itself and needs to be practiced diligently.

Now you may be asking yourself, "What is the best way to improve my aerial kicking skills?" If you are, then you need to immediately go back to page number nine and read it again!

Awards & Accomplishments

This is a picture of the first world record certificate that I received from the Guinness Book of World Records for performing 10,502 High Kicks in 5 hours and 30 minutes on September 27, 1986 in Butte, Montana USA.

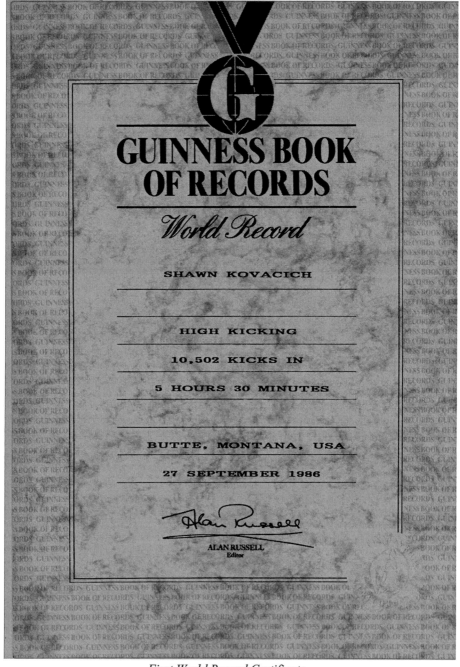

GUINNESS BOOK OF RECORDS

World Record

SHAWN KOVACICH

HIGH KICKING

10,502 KICKS IN

5 HOURS 30 MINUTES

BUTTE, MONTANA, USA

27 SEPTEMBER 1986

ALAN RUSSELL
Editor

First World Record Certificate

This is a picture of the second world record certificate that I received from the Guinness Book of World Records for performing 11,000 High Kicks in 5 hours 18 minutes and 43 seconds on January 21, 1989 in Anaconda, Montana USA.

Second World Record Certificate

This is a picture of the actual letter that I received from The Guinness Book of World Records officially recognizing my second world record for performing 11,000 High Kicks in 5 hours 18 minutes and 43 seconds on January 21, 1989 in Anaconda, Montana USA.

GUINNESS BOOK OF RECORDS

Mr S Kovacich   17 March 1989
211B Main
Anaconda
MT 59711
USA

Dear Mr Kovacich

Thank you for sending us the two signed statements as requested in our letter of 21 February.

We are now in a position to recognise your achievement as a new record, and unless we receive details of a better claim before we go to press, your record will be included in the 1990 book. As mentioned in our letter, however, it is a category which will be dropped after next year's book.

Enclosed is a certificate in recognition of your record - congratulations.

Yours sincerely

Nicholas Heath-Brown

Nicholas Heath-Brown
Deputy Editor

33 London Road, Enfield, Middlesex EN2 6DJ. England. Tel: 01-367 4567 Telex: 23573 GBR LDN Fax: 01 367 5912
Guinness Publishing Ltd, Registered Office: 39 Portman Square, London, W1H 9HB. Registered: London 2079632

The above photograph was taken of me delivering a kick to one of my opponents during a match at the prestigious Sabaki Challenge, which is held annually in Denver, Colorado.

This is another photograph taken of me fighting against one of my opponents during a match at the prestigious Sabaki Challenge, which is held annually in Denver, Colorado.

Sneak Preview

Achieving Kicking Excellence; Volume Four: Front Kick

Preview of Volume Six: Front Kick

The Back Leg Front Kick is one of the ten primary kicks associated mainly with Karate and Tae Kwon Do. This kicked is delivered with a straight forward type motion and relies more on speed and momentum for power, rather than actual physical strength. The striking surface utilized in the delivery of this kick is the ball of the foot. However, the effects of a Front Kick are greatly reduced when any other part of the foot other than the ball of the foot, is utilized. However, under special circumstances, the preferred striking implement will be the bottom of the heel rather than the ball of the foot.

The Front Kick, along with the Roundhouse Kick, is one of the most versatile kicks you can use. The Front Kick can literally be used to strike almost anywhere on your opponent's body, from the nose to the ankle and almost every vital or vulnerable point in between. Although there are several major factors involved in the correct execution of a Front Kick, one of the most important is the proper foot positioning of your kicking leg foot prior to impact. Many a student has succumbed to unnecessary foot and ankle injuries due to a lack of understanding and improper foot positioning when executing the Front Kick.

Depending upon how it is used, the Front Kick is not by its very nature a very powerful kick, I feel that it is better suited as a set-up technique to be used on your opponent prior to delivering a finishing technique. Similar to how a boxer uses his jab to set-up the more powerful right cross and/or hook punch. The Front Kick, like the Crescent Kick and Reverse Crescent Kick, are relatively easy to learn and are often some of the first kicks a student will learn. Although they are not the most powerful kicks, they are still very effective when used correctly.

In order to obtain the maximum amount of impact potential in the Front Kick, your base leg, kicking leg, hips, and upper body have to be utilized correctly throughout the entire kicking sequence.

Pictorial Overview:

Fighting Position

Raise Knee

Coil

Midway to Impact

Impact

Recoil

Position #1

Position #2

Recommended Reading

Basic Anatomy of the Reverse Crescent Kick

1. Rasch, Philip J. Ph.D. & Burke, Roger K. Ph.D., Kinesiology and Applied Anatomy, (Lea & Febiger, Philadelphia, Pennsylvania, 1978)

2. Gray, Henry F.R.S., Gray's Anatomy, (Running Press, Philadelphia, Pennsylvania, 1974)

Warm Up and Stretching

1. Anderson, Bob, Stretching, (Shelter Publications, Inc., Bolinas, California, 1980)

Basic Principles of Kicking Movement

1. Fixx, James E., Maximum Sports Performance, (Random House, Inc., New York and Toronto, 1985)

2. Loehr, James E., Ed.D., Mental Toughness Training for Sports, (Stephen Greene Press, Inc., 1986)

3. Mashiro, N., Ph.D., Black Medicine: The Dark Art of Death, (Paladin Press, Boulder, Colorado, 1978)

4. Brancazio, Peter J., Sport Science, (Touchstone/Simon & Schuster, Inc., New York, New York, 1985)

5. Adams, Brian, Deadly Karate Blows: The Medical Implications, (Unique Publications, Burbank, California, 1985)

6. Hibbard, Jack, Karate Breaking Techniques: with Practical Applications, (Charles E. Tuttle Company, Inc., Tokyo, Japan, 1981)

Training and Practice Methods

1. Urquidez, Benny "The Jet", Training and Fighting Skills, (Unique Publications, Inc., Burbank, California, 1981)

2. Derse, Ed, Explosive Power-Plyometrics for Bodybuilders, Martial Artists & other Athletes, (Health for Life, Los Angeles, California, 1993)

3. Secrets of Advanced Body Builders, (Health For Life, Los Angeles, California, 1985)

4. Simon, Ilene Caryn, Mind Gains, (Health For Life, Los Angeles, California, 1995)

5. Robinson, Jerry & Carrino, Frank, Max 02 The Complete Guide To Synergistic Aerobic Training, (Health For Life, Los Angeles, California, 1993)

6. The Human Fuel Handbook, (Health For Life, Los Angeles, California, 1988)

Martial Arts & Self-Defense

1. Van Schuyver, Mark & Villalobos, Kru Pedro Solana, Fighting Strategies of Muay Thai, (Paladin Press, Boulder, Colorado, 2002)

2. Boykin, Chad, Muay Thai Kickboxing, (Paladin Press, Boulder, Colorado, 2002)

3. Rielly, Robin L., Karate Training, (Charles E. Tuttle, Co., Rutland, Vermont, 1985)

4. Reid, Howard, & Croucher, Michael, The Way of the Warrior, (The Overlook Press, Woodstock, New York, 1983)

5. Bolelli, Daniele, On the Warrior's Path, (Frog, Ltd., Berkeley, California, 2003)

6. Beaumont, Ned, The Savage Science of Street Fighting, (Paladin Press, Boulder, Colorado, 2001)

7. Urban, Peter, The Karate Sensei, (Masters Publication, Hamilton, Ontario, 1984)

8. Delp, Christoph, Muay Thai: Advanced Kickboxing Techniques, (Frog, Ltd., Berkeley, California, 2004)

INDEX

E

Eight Directions of Attack, 137
elbows, 27
elbow techniques, 140, 159
end of arc, 52-54
environment, 136
equilibrium, 28-29
excessive force, 27
explosive, 80, 111, 186
extensor digitorum longus, 14-22
extensor hallucis longus, 14-22
external oblique, 14-22
extreme caution, 26
eye contact, 31, 65

F

facial area, 27
feather, 186
femur, 11-14
femur, head of the, 11-14
fibula, 11-14
Fields, Joe, 34
fighting stance, 35-38
figure skater, 28
firing pin, 94
flashlight, 31, 36
flexibility, 23-24, 136
flexor digitorum longus, 14-22
fluid motion, 114, 122
follow through, 33, 49-51
foot position, 30, 46
footwork, 86, 112, 118, 138, 191
force = mass x acceleration, 177
force bag, 177
Foreman, George, 28
foundation, 63
Front Kick, 104, 143, 204
Front Leg Reverse Crescent Kick, 116-123

G

gastrocnemius, 14-22
gemelli, 14-22
gi pants, 88
giraffe, 28

glabella, 27
gluteus maximus, 14-22
gluteus medius, 14-22
gracilis, 14-22
grappling, 29, 140, 159
gravel, 28
Guinness Book of World Records, 5, 200-202
gunpowder, 94-95

H

hammer(ing), 26, 188
hand techniques, 140, 159
hanging, 78, 183
height, 28
high section, 76
hippopotamus, 28
Hop/Slide Backward Reverse Crescent Kick, 108-115
Hop/Slide Forward Reverse Crescent Kick, 100-107
house, 63
hub, 106
human factor, 26
Hunn, Ben, 5

I

ice, 28
iliopsoas, 14-22
iliotibial tract, 14-22
impact, 33, 45-48
inclined leg press, 163-164
innate response, 119
instinctive, 10, 31

J

jam, 33, 112
jaw, 27, 32, 146, 186
joint techniques, 140, 157, 159
jump rope, 176
Jump Turning Reverse Crescent Kick, 144-151

K

Karate, 5, 35, 204

Kiaa, 156
kicking paddle, 177
Knechtges, Brian, 5
knee, 11-14, 27, 80
knee joint, 11-14
knee strikes, 140
Kovacich, Shawn, 5

L

Lamborghini, 32-33
laser beam, 31
Lee, Bruce, 4, 24
left leg, 7, 152-160
long range, 140
low section, 76
lower arms, 27
lower legs, 27
lunges, 173

M

mathematical level, 9
maximum effectiveness, 31
metatarsals, 11-14
mid range, 140
midsection, 76
mirror & tape, 161
mouth, 27
muscles, 14-22
muscular control, 31-32

N

nail, 26, 126, 188
navicular, 11-14
neck area, 27
nose, 27
Nurmi, Paavo, 34

O

occipital bone, 27
Off-Setting Turning Reverse Crescent Kick, 133-143
optimum level, 175
optimum results, 111
orbital bones, 27
outer rim, 106

over-extend(ing), 30, 86

P

patella, 11-14
path of trajectory, 40, 43, 47, 50, 53, 95, 98, 131
pavement, 28
peak of arc, 42-44
pectineus, 14-22
pelvic girdle, 11-14
pelvis, 11-14
pelvis, acetabulum of the, 11-14
penetrating impact, 26
pennies, 183
peripheral vision, 31, 36
peroneus brevis, 14-22
peroneus longus, 14-22
peroneus tertius, 14-22
phalanges, 11-14
philtrum, 27
pivot(ing), 30, 32, 70-71, 75, 80, 93, 139
plantaris, 14-22
plyometrics, 171-172, 175
pocketwatch, 191
point of chin, 27
popliteal region, 14-22
positive thinking, 34
power, 32, 177-178
practice, 10, 31
pressure per square inch, 25-26
primary kick, 35-62
primer, 94
proper principles, 78
proper repetitive practice, 176
punch(ing), 29, 140, 157
push, 25-26, 97

Q

quadriceps, 14-22
quality supervision, 10
quick draw, 175, 177
Quinn, Michael, 163

tree, 130
trigger, 94
trouble shooting, 179-181
Turning Reverse Crescent Kick, 63-72

U

USTU, 5

V

variations, 63-160
vastus lateralis, 14-22
vastus medialis, 14-22
visualization, 34
vital point, 26-27, 89, 97, 143, 185-186
vulnerable, 78
vulnerable point, 26-27, 89, 97, 143,
185-186

W

wagon wheel, 106
warm-up, 9, 23-24
water training, 176, 178
weak leg, 154
weight, 28
weight lifting belt, 167
weight lifting gloves, 167
wobble, 149
wood, 26
wrist, 27

Y

Y, 150

Notes:

Notes:

Notes:

Notes:

Notes:

Notes:

Notes:

Notes: